A PRACTICAL GUIDE TO PRAYER

Olubi Johnson

A PRACTICAL GUIDE TO PRAYER

© 1988 Olubi Johnson
First Published March, 1987 by
SCRIPTURE PASTURE CHRISTIAN CENTRE

ISBN: 978-978-57224-1-3

This Revised Edition Published September, 2019

CHRIST LIFE MINISTRIES

U.I.P.O. Box 20923,
Ibadan, Nigeria.

+234-805-226-6794, +234-805-506-1415

e-mail: scripturepasture@spcconline.org
Internet: www.spcconline.net

All Scripture quotations are from the Authorized King James Version unless otherwise stated.

National Library of Nigeria cataloguing in publication data.

Published by: Epignosis Publications Limited, Ibadan, Nigeria

Preface

In order to use this book and the prayers in it successfully, one must be a born again Christian. To be born again, one must believe that Jesus died for his sins and has been raised from the dead.

Doing this will cause our sins to be forgiven by God, and cause an inner transformation in our hearts that will make us Godlike in nature. It is this change of heart, through recognition and repentance (turning away from) of a past life of sin and accepting Jesus Christ as Lord and Saviour to begin a new life of righteousness that is called being born again.

If you have never experienced this change of heart through consciously and deliberately inviting Jesus Christ into your heart and life you can do so now by saying with sincerity the following prayer:

Dear Father God in Heaven,
I come to you in the name of Jesus and I know you will not cast me out.
I realize I have the nature of sin inside me because I inherited it from my parents, from Adam and Eve in the Garden of Eden; but I do not want this nature of sin to continue to dominate me.

So I believe Jesus died for my sins and shed His blood for the forgiveness, cleansing and wiping away of all my sins.

I also believe that Jesus Christ was raised up from the dead for my justification.

So I accept Him as my Saviour and confess Him as my Lord. Therefore now I am born-again by having God's nature, eternal life, living water in my heart as a seed.

Father, I thank You for this. Teach me Your ways, show me Lord how to love and serve You and I determine in my heart not to go back to a regular life of sin but rather to serve You in righteousness and holiness all the days of my life. Even if I sin, I will quickly repent and continue in righteousness.

I will look after this seed of Your life and nature inside me and let it grow into the fullness of Christ in Jesus Name.

For further details see or write for our book, "The Why and How of Being Born Again."

Introduction

This book you are about to read is just what the title says it is, "A Practical Guide to Prayer." In order to use it properly you need to understand the importance and the place of prayer in the life of men.

Prayer basically is the communication of information and power between man in the physical realm and God in the spiritual realm. Man cannot live successfully or victoriously independent of God, for "in Him we live and move and have our being" (Acts 17: 28). Prayer is the avenue through which we draw the necessary resources from God for successful and victorious living. The reason so many people in the world today fail in life is because they do not know how to pray. They do not know how to contact God and get the necessary information and power from Him to overcome the problems of life, which in reality have a spiritual origin, by the limited understanding of the human mind and by natural human power.

Since the problems of life basically are spiritual in origin, the human methods of solution fail and reality seems to elude us. However, through prayer we can tap into God's unlimited resources to solve the problems of life.

Prayer as revealed in the bible is rather technical, in that it is governed by certain principles, which, if violated, will cause the prayer to be ineffective.

Thus prayer is an art (or science if you like) that must be studied and then put into constant practice to produce effective results.

This book does not attempt to go into exposition of the principles of prayer (that is a whole subject in itself) rather, it simply gives prayers and guidelines of how they should be used.

These prayers are based on principles revealed **in the word of God,** the bible and have been found to work and produce results in real life.

The idea behind this book is to give the Christian, a prayer guide which he can immediately put into practice and begin to see results, even before he fully understands all the principles behind the prayers. I believe that the best way to learn is by practice. Of course at the same time one is practicing the art of prayer, one will also be studying the principles that govern prayer in the bible and by the combination of practice and study, one will become a proficient prayer warrior through whom God can do His work of destroying the works of the devil and blessing men.

The book starts with explaining the importance of the life and power of God in relation to prayer and how to draw this life and power from God. This is the foundation upon which all prayer is effective.

The other chapters tell us what prayers you can make and how to say them in different situations (e.g. there are prayers for healing, prosperity and deliverance). There is a chapter on the Holy Spirit and prayer and it shows how the power of the Holy Spirit in your life can make your prayer life more powerful and effective. There is also a chapter on a practical guide to daily prayer, which shows you how to use the different prayers in your daily prayer life for victorious Christian living. All you need to do is simply read through and then obey step by step, the instructions given on how to pray and you will begin to see results and have a deeper understanding of the Bible and God. It is good to add that the prayers shown here indicate typical or model prayers based on principles.

They are not formulae to be adhered to rigidly. Rather, they exemplify principles, which if adhered to in sincerity will produce results in your life to the glory of God.

The first edition of this book was written in 1987; this new edition has a few alterations and additions based on new and clearer revelation of some of the principles of prayer in chapter 2 on the Holy Spirit and prayer and revelation knowledge, And in chapter 5 on daily, weekly and monthly prayers for the Christian. I trust that as you begin to live a life of prayer, through the guidelines and prayers in this book, God's blessings will be manifest in your life helping you overcome the difficulties of life and transforming you more and more into the likeness of Jesus Christ.
God bless you as you read and pray.

Love in Christ Jesus
Olubi Johnson
March 1987

Table of Contents

Introduction to the Life and Power Scriptures

1

WHAT THE LIFE OF GOD IS

In John 5:26 we read
For as the Father hath life in Himself; so hath He given to the Son to have life in Himself.

And in John 1:4
In Him was life and the life was the light of men.

And in 1 John 5:11-12
And this is the record that God hath given to us eternal life and this life is in His Son. (12) He that hath the Son hath life and he that hath not the Son hath not life.

The Greek word translated life or everlasting life in these scriptures is the word 'Zoe'. It is the spiritual substance in God that makes God, God. Just as blood is the substance in you, that makes you a living physical being, Zoe is the substance in God that makes Him a living spiritual being. This life is called everlasting because it is unending in its quality.

Simply put, eternal life is the spiritual substance that God has in Him. It is the spiritual substance inside God that makes Him, God! It is literally a spiritual living water which flows inside God like blood flows in the physical body. Just as the blood flowing in you makes you a living physical being, Zoe flowing in God makes Him a living spiritual being (Leviticus 17:11).

Zoe is called everlasting because it is unending in its quantity inside God. Zoe eternal life is the life that God uses to create and sustain all that exists. It originates from Him, sustains all creation and circulates back to Him in a cycle so that it is unending in God.

Romans 11:36
For of (originating in) Him, and through Him (sustaining all creation), and to (circulating back to) Him, are all things: to whom be glory for ever. Amen.

Practically what this means is that if God (hypothetically) had a certain measure, say 100 measures, of Zoe and then He released from Himself, 5 measures, logically, there should remain 95 measures in Him.

However, because of the unending or eternal quality of Zoe one will find that God would have 100 or even more measures of Zoe in Him.
This is because as Zoe is expended more of it is automatically recycled. This is what makes God, God, what makes Him eternal, what makes Him unfathomable.

Now this life is what was in Jesus when He was on earth as a man. (See John 5:26 above). This Zoe was in His spirit. It is this same Zoe that came into our spirits when we believed in Jesus the Son of God, and were born again. In fact, it was the entry of this Zoe into our spirits that recreated our spirits, and made us new creatures in Christ Jesus (See John 1: 4 and 1 John 5:10-12).

CONTINUING IN LIFE
Now in 2 Peter 1:3 - 4, we read;
According as His divine power hath given unto us all things that pertain unto life and godliness, through the knowledge of Him that hath called us to glory and virtue. Whereby are given unto us exceedingly great and precious promises: that by these ye might be partakers of the divine nature, having escaped the corruption that is in the world through lust.

It is this same Zoe that is spoken of in verses 3 and 4. Peter tells us even after we have been born again, we can still continue to receive this Zoe into our beings through the knowledge of the exceeding great and precious promises of God in the Bible, that promise us this Zoe. It is essential for every Christian to appreciate what Zoe is, and why it is necessary to continue to have its flow into your spirit, soul and body throughout your Christian life. Also it is necessary to see how the amount of Zoe in your spirit, soul and body determines how successfully you can walk in the Spirit and get answers to prayer.

In John 15:5 the scripture says:
I am the vine, ye are the branches.

Here the scripture paints a vivid picture of us being vitally united or connected to Christ our Lord.

Functionally, this implies that there is to be a continuous flow of God's life from Christ (the Vine) to us (the branches).

The scripture in 2 Peter 1:3, 4 above tells us that there are promises (and sometimes just statements of fact which can be acted upon in faith, just as promises are claimed by faith) which will produce or give to us this Zoe itself primarily and that will also produce godliness. Godliness is Godlikeness and is the manifestation of the nature and character of God. It is the presence of Zoe in great measure in the human spirit, soul and body, that will lead to the manifestation of the nature and character of God in our daily conduct and experience.
There are:
(i)   Promises (e.g. Philippians 4:19)
(ii)   Commandments (e.g. John 13:34) and
(iii)   Statements of fact (e.g. 1Peter 2:24) made in scripture, which when believed, confessed and acted upon produce godliness in the life of a Christian.

What is essential to see is that no confession of any promise, commandment or statement to produce godliness will be effectual or creative unless the heart is full of Zoe. When we speak God's words of promise, commandment or statement of fact, those words will be creative and effectual only if our hearts or spirits are full of Zoe.

WORDS AND LIFE

When we speak or confess words, our words contain spiritual substance. This spiritual substance could either be good or bad. Words are containers or vehicles through which spiritual power is released into the physical world.

John 6:63
The words that I speak unto you, they are spirit and they are life.

If our spirits or hearts are full of Zoe then our words will also be full of Zoe It is because God is full of Zoe that God's words are living and powerful. For this reason what God says becomes a physical reality. This is shown in Hebrews 4:12 and Luke 1:37:

Hebrews 4:12
For the word of God is living and powerful sharper than any two-edged sword.....

Luke 1:37 (Worrell's Translation)
... because no word from God shall be without power.

The reason why some Christians speak or confess God's Word and get very little or no result is because their hearts are not full of Zoe and so their words are not powerful. To speak or confess God's Word and get results, one must have his heart full of Zoe. This is why God says in John 15:7:

If ye abide in me, and my words (remember His words are life; see John 6: 63 above) abide in you, you shall ask what you will, and it shall be done unto you.

In Luke 6:45 we read;
A good man out of the good treasure of his heart bringeth forth that which is good; and an evil man out of the evil treasure in his heart bringeth forth that which is evil: for of the abundance of the heart his mouth speaketh.

The good treasure that will bring forth the good things of godliness is Zoe This is also true of praying in other tongues or praying in the Spirit (I Corinthians 14:2). If the heart is not full of Zoe, the praying will not be spiritually effective (I Corinthians 13:4). So we see that the constant flow of Zoe into our spirits and then into our souls and bodies is an essential and foundational prerequisite for victorious Christian living and effectual prayer life.

THE LIFE AND POWER SCRIPTURES
The specific scriptures that either promise or state that Zoe is available to us are what we call the Life and Power scriptures. All scriptures that promise life, power and strength essentially promise Zoe.

It is important here to see that the constant flow of Zoe in our spirits, souls and bodies is not automatic. Rather it will only occur as we consciously and deliberately exercise faith in the Word of God that promises Zoe. This is true of everything we have from God. For example healing is ours, but it does not flow automatically until we deliberately and consciously exercise faith in healing scriptures. Also prosperity is ours, but it does not come to us automatically until we deliberately exercise faith in God's Word on prosperity.

13

The Zoe we received when we got born again is constantly being expended and so if we do not receive more of it deliberately by faith in God's Word that promises it, we will be in a place where the amount of life in us is very small and so we will not see the fruit of the Spirit or divine wisdom and power in our lives to any appreciable degree. It is not that the life of God in us will be completely exhausted and dry up; that can only happen if we reject Christ and are cut off from the Body (John 15: 6). However, the amount of life in us will be so small that our Christian lives will not be fruitful to any significant degree, our understanding of scriptures will be darkened and we will not have any deep and intimate fellowship with God.

This has been the situation in generations of Christians since the days of the early apostles and so there has been little spiritual growth and development in the church in terms of fruit, divine wisdom and understanding and power. Thank God in our generation we have the priviledge to have an insight into these life scriptures so that we can have life more abundantly as God desires that we should (John 10:10).

MEASURES OF LIFE
We also need to understand that just as you cannot eat one 'almighty' meal and not be hungry for the rest of your life, neither can you do the same for eternal life. The manna the children of Israel received in the wilderness was daily, and each man went out to collect what he could carry daily. In the same way we must receive life from God by faith daily, and what each man is able to receive varies according to our different spiritual capacities (receiving life will be discussed in detail later).

THE DAYS OF IGNORANCE
You may ask the question 'If receiving eternal life by faith daily is so essential, how is it that the 99 percent of the Church who

14

are ignorant of this have not perished?' This is because in the days of ignorance God winked (Acts 17:30) and we need to understand that you receive eternal life every time you fellowship with God, because God is life personified.

This means any Christian who simply loves to pray and read his bible daily will receive eternal life and refreshing from the presence of the Lord, even though he may not be aware of what is happening precisely.

This can be compared to a man leaving an empty bucket out in the open. Every time it rains or even when the dew falls every morning he is sure to collect a certain amount of water; however the amount collected will be limited and can easily be contaminated by impurities (like bird droppings) from the open environment. Conversely, water that is pumped deliberately from a well or river through pipes and purified will be both pure and in abundance.

So Christians who get the life of God without the knowledge and faith of deliberately drawing life from God through the scriptures receive a limited amount of life, which can easily be contaminated by sin and demonic forces because of their ignorance or carelessness. However, Jesus did not just come to give us eternal life, but He came to give it to us more abundantly (John 10:10). This scripture has not yet been fulfilled in the Church, but we are now living in the days of its fulfilment. It therefore, becomes necessary for God to restore the understanding of how to consciously and deliberately receive eternal life by faith. This is like taking that bucket to or pumping water from the well instead of just leaving it in the open and waiting for rain or dew.

DRAWING LIFE
Isaiah 12:3
Therefore with joy you will draw water from the wells of salvation. (NKJV)

15

Drawing life from God using the exceeding great and precious promises is a technical thing (spiritually speaking). We can use the natural example of the physical body to illustrate this spiritual truth. Your physical heart pumps blood to circulate around the body. In exactly the same way your born again spirit is a spiritual pump which pumps life. Jesus said:

John 4:14
But whoever drinks of the water that I shall give him will never thirst. But the water that I shall give him will become in him a fountain of water springing up into everlasting life. (NKJV)

Jesus is telling this woman that He has come to give her spiritual water (life), and that if she believes in Him that spiritual water will create in her a well spring of life. The contemporary equivalent of this would be a pump connected to a well of everlasting life that you can always activate at will. The Lord Jesus is the well and your spirit is the pump-reservoir. If you are born again then you have been connected to the well and there is no need for you to ever thirst again. Many Christians are thirsting today, however, because they are not consciously pumping from the well. This same truth can be seen in the illustration the Lord Jesus gave of the vine and the branches.

John 15:4-5
I am the vine, you are the branches. He who abides in me, and I in him, bears much fruit; for without me you can do nothing. (NKJV)

The vine is the source of life from which the branches all tap. The branches that tap the most life will produce the most fruit, while those that do not tap at all will wither and die; or atrophy. Using the great and precious promises you can pump spiritual water from the well (or vine) into your spirit (reservoir), and from your spirit to your soul, to your physical body and into your circumstances.

HOW DO WE PUMP?

Basically what you must do is to take the promise, believe it in your heart and confess it with your mouth. When you do this, your heart acts like a pump and draws life from the well (Jesus via the Holy Spirit) into your heart, from where it can flow up to the rest of your system.
Infact your spirit or inner man pumps Zoe just like your physical heart pumps blood.

Proverbs 18:20-21
A man's belly shall be satisfied with the fruit of his mouth; and with the increase of his lips shall he be filled. Death and life are in the power of the tongue: and they that love it shall eat the fruit thereof.

The belly here refers to the human spirit. God wants our bellies to be filled with life all the time, and this must be done by praying from many life scriptures ("... the increase of his lips... " i.e. many confessions). The more scriptures which promise life that you confess, the greater the amount of God's life and power that is deposited in your spirit, soul and body.
Each time you pray from a life scripture you will receive a measure of life. This is another concept that is unknown to many Christians. Life is not ministered all at once, but in measures, and the size of these measures increase as you grow spiritually.

Romans 12:3
"For I say, through the grace given unto me, to every man that is among you, not to think of himself more highly than he ought to think; but to think soberly, according as God hath dealt to every man the measure of faith."

When you want to eat dinner you cannot swallow the whole meal in one gulp, you must eat it in mouth fulls. The mouth full of a small child will be smaller than the mouth full of an adult.

Also the full capacity of the small child's belly will be smaller than the full capacity of an adult's belly. Everything in God is a gradual process. The bible says the measure of the capacity of our hearts can be enlarged: Psalms 119:32; 2Corinthians 10:13; 2Corinthians 10:15.

SPIRITUAL WORK
Proverbs 10:16
The labour of the righteous tendeth to life: the fruit of the wicked to sin.

Drawing life is spiritual labour, and if you are baptised in the Holy Spirit you are better equipped for that labour. The difference between a person baptised in the Holy Spirit and one who is not is that one draws water with a pump (John 7:37-38) while the other draws with a bucket. It is the efficiency that differs.

Whether you use the pump or the bucket illustration, however, the principle is the same. The scripture promise is represented by the bucket (or the pipe connecting the well to the pump), the life of God is represented by the water in the well, and your mouth or tongue is represented by the rope (or the pump switch). Your human spirit can be seen as the pump-reservoir which is filled by pumping water from the well, and which supplies water to the soul, body and circumstances.

To draw life you must tie the rope to the bucket (switch on the motor). Then you must throw the bucket into the well and make sure it hits the water and is filled with water (the pump must be primed) before you draw it up. This tells us that the labour of faith needed to draw life is one that requires more than just a mechanical recital of the life scriptures.

It requires you to concentrate when you are praying from any particular scripture, and visualise (see by faith) the flow of life as it

. flows from the well via the pump into the reservoir, and into your soul, body and circumstances, according to the specifics of each scripture

When life is drawn mechanically it is akin to the bucket not being allowed to hit the water before it is drawn up, or perhaps the bucket is not filled properly (or the pump is not primed). Another hindrance to efficient drawing of life is your attitude towards those in spiritual authority over you. The bible says:

1 Peter 5:5
Likewise you younger people, submit yourselves to your elders. Yes, all of you be submissive to one another, and be clothed with humility; for God resists the proud, But gives grace to the humble. (NKJV)

If you do not have an attitude of honesty and humility towards those in authority then God will resist you, and you will not be able to draw life efficiently. But when you have an honest and an humble heart, God's mercy and grace will be available to you, and you will find that in all your spiritual labours His yoke will be easy and His burden light.

So in praying to ask God to minister His life and power to our spirits and souls and bodies; we base these requests on certain specific scriptures:

2Peter 1:3,4
According as his divine power hath given unto us all things that pertain unto life and godliness through the knowledge of him that hath called us to glory and virtue: Whereby are given unto us exceeding great and precious promises that by these ye might be partakers of the divine nature, having escaped the corruption that is in the world through lust.

We can base our faith on the principles of receiving life, power, strength, love and wisdom by exercising faith in specific scriptures. According to Mark 11:22-24:

Have faith in God…. For verily I say unto you that whosoever shall say unto this mountain, be thou removed, and be thou cast into the sea, and shall not doubt in his heart, but shall believe that those things which he saith shall come to pass, he shall have whatsoever he saith. Therefore I say unto you, what things soever ye desire, when ye pray, believe that ye receive them and ye shall have them.

And Romans 10:9-10
That if thou shalt confess with thy mouth the Lord Jesus, and shalt believe in thine heart that God hath raised him from the dead, thou shalt be saved. For with the heart man believeth unto righteousness, and with the mouth confession is made unto salvation.
So, briefly, the way to pray or make confessions on the Word of God is to:
(1)   Quote the specific scriptures to yourself.
(2)   Make a personal prayer or confession based on that scripture.
(3)   Believe that what you have asked for or confessed is true immediately you say it.
(4)   Act like it is true irrespective of your feelings and circumstances.

It is important to realize that each time we confess or pray a scripture for life, a certain measure of eternal life or God's power is deposited into our spirits, souls and bodies. By confessing these scriptures constantly, we can have an abundant amount of God's life and power in us, or have it without measure as Christ did.

John 3:34
For he whom God hath sent speaketh the words of God, for God giveth not the Spirit by measure unto him.

John 10:10
... I am come that they might have life, and that they might have it more abundantly.

It is for this reason we use as many scriptures as possible to draw life from the Lord. Here are a few examples of such prayers and confessions and the expected results

Please note that as you pray, your focus should be on God. You should visualize yourself as a branch of the vine, drawing life from the vine. It is for this reason you close your eyes when you pray, So that your mind will be fixed on what you are praying about and you will see yourself drawing life and power from God (see illustration on inside back cover of this book).

Also, it is good and right to always acknowledge and reverence God (Father, Son and Holy Spirit), especially the Holy Spirit, as it is He who gives life, before you start praying. It is not the Word we draw life from, but rather we draw life from God through the Word.

Scripture: John 16:23: "And in that day ye shall ask me nothing. Verily, verily I say unto you, whatsoever ye shall ask the Father in my name he will give it you."

Prayer: Father, I strip myself of every confidence I might have in my knowledge or ability to pray. I place all my confidence in Your mercies, the grace of the Lord Jesus and the help of the Holy Spirit as I pray now in Jesus name.

Result:	The Lord ministers to you mercy to be faithful, grace to be humble and the help of the Holy Spirit to pray to receive life from God without leaning upon your own knowledge or ability.
*Scripture:	John 10:10 "… I am come that they might have life and that they might have it more abundantly."
Prayer:	Father, give life to my spirit now, and that in a measure that is more than enough to enable me to pray effectually and fervently to receive life and power from God through the word, in Jesus Name.
Result:	A measure of God's life, more than enough to meet the particular needs you will presently face in prayer is sent to your spirit.
*Scripture:	Ephesians 3:16-19: "That He (God) would grant you, according to the riches of His glory, to be strengthened with might by His Spirit, in the inner man. That Christ may dwell in your hearts by faith; that ye being rooted and grounded in love, may be able to comprehend with all saints what is the breadth, and length, and depth, height; and to know the love of Christ, which passeth knowledge, that ye might be filled with all the fullness of God."
Prayer:	Father, we pray that you grant us according to the riches of Your glory to be more strengthened with might by Your Spirit in the inner man so that Christ would dwell more in your hearts by faith; that we become more rooted and grounded in love, that we may be able to comprehend more with all saints what is the breadth, and length, and depth, and the height of the body of Christ; and so to know the love of Christ, which surpaasses knowledge, that we might be filled with all the fullness of God in Jesus Name.

22

Result: A measure of God's power is sent into your spirit to be able to draw life so that the life of God will constantly flow in your soul, causing you to be strengthened with might by God's Spirit to draw life effectively as you pray.

*Scripture: Colossians 1:11: "Strengthened with all might according to his glorious power, unto all patience and longsuffering with joyfulness."

Prayer: Father, strengthen me with all might according to Your glorious power unto all patience and longsuffering with joyfulness as I go into prayer now in Jesus' Name. Amen.

Result: A measure of God's power is sent into your spirit, soul and body causing you to be patient (or steadfast and consistent) and full of joy and forbearance in your prayer life and walk in the Spirit.

*Scripture: John 10:27 "My sheep hear my voice, and I know them, and they follow me."

Prayer: Lord, You are my Shepherd. I hear Your voice and I follow You as I pray now, in Jesus Name. Amen

Result: A measure of God's power is sent into your spirit, this enables you to be sensitive to the Spirit. It also enables you to obey His voice.

*Scripture: Isaiah 40:31 "But they that wait upon the Lord shall renew their strength, they shall mount up with wings as eagles; they shall run, and not be weary; and they shall walk, and not faint."

Prayer:	Father, I am serving You with my spirit. Renew now the strength of my spirit, causing me to be stronger than all wicked spirits in heavenly places, so that I will run, and not be weary, and walk and not faint in Jesus Name. Amen.
Result:	A measure of God's power or strength is sent to your spirit, making you to be stronger than all wicked spirits in the heavenly places. Thus as you engage and wrestle them in prayer, you will overcome them. Also this strength will make you run and not be weary and walk and not faint spiritually and physically, until when you have used all the strength and you need to pray again for more strength.
Scripture:	Psalm 18:28 "For thou wilt light my candle, the Lord my God will enlighten my darkness."
Prayer:	Father, thank You for lighting my candle (i.e. getting me born again). Enlighten my darkness further now by Your life in Jesus Name. Amen.
Result:	The result of this prayer is that a measure of God's life which contains His light is sent from Christ, through your spirit to focus on your mind, bringing enlightenment and understanding.
Scripture:	Psalm 18:32 "It is God that girdeth me with strength and maketh my way perfect."
Prayer:	Father, gird me with strength in my heart (spirit and soul) and body and so make my way perfect in Jesus Name. Amen.

Result: The result of this prayer is that a measure of God's strength or power is sent to focus on your spirit, soul and body which will strengthen any weakness therein. This will help you make less mistakes in your conduct due to weakness in your spirit, soul and body.

Scripture: Psalm 18:39 "For thou hast girded me with strength unto the battle; thou hast subdued under me those that rose up against me."

Prayer: Father, gird me with strength in my heart (spirit and soul) and body unto the battle of faith and prayer as I go into prayer now, in Jesus Name. Amen.

Result: A measure of God's power is sent by the Holy Spirit to your spirit, soul and body to enable you to overcome satan and his cohorts as you wrestle them in faith and prayer.

Scripture: Psalm 119:25 "My soul cleaveth unto the dust, quicken thou me according to thy word."

Prayer: Father, give life to me according to Your Word, so that my soul will not cleave unto the dust in Jesus Name. Amen

Result: A measure of God's life flows into your soul, particularly your will, to make your will align with God's will and purposes.

Scripture: Psalm 119:28 "My soul melteth for heaviness, strengthen thou me according to thy word."

Prayer: Father, strengthen me according to Thy Word so that my soul will not drop (or melt) for heaviness in Jesus Name. Amen.

Result: A measure of God's strength or power is sent through your spirit from Christ to focus on your will in your soul.

Scripture: Psalm 119:32 "I will run the way of thy commandments, when thou shalt enlarge my heart."

Prayer: Father, enlarge my heart, so that I will run the way of Thy commandments in Jesus Name. Amen.

Result: A measure of God's life is sent from the Lord through your spirit to focus on your will, increasing its capacity to endure the will of God willingly even when it is very difficult to do so, humanly speaking. An excellent example of this happening is when Christ was strengthened in prayer at Gethsemane, just before He went to the cross (Luke 22:40-46).

Scripture: Psalm 119:35 "Make me to go in the path of thy commandments, for therein do I delight."

Prayer: Father, direct me in the path of Thy commandments for therein do I delight in Jesus Name. Amen.

Result: A measure of God's life and power is sent to your mind and will, making it possible to know and to do the will of God.

Scripture: Psalm 119:36 "Incline my heart unto thy testimonies, and not to covetousness."

Prayer: Father, incline my heart (my soul, my desires) unto Thy testimonies and not to covetousness in Jesus Name. Amen.

Result: A measure of God's life is sent from God through your spirit to focus on your soul, in particular on your desires and emotions. This makes you desire and love the things of God and not the carnal things of this world.

Scripture: Psalm 119:37 "Turn away mine eyes from beholding vanity and quicken thou (or give life to) me in thy way."

Prayer: Father, turn away mine eyes from beholding vanity and give life to me in Thy way in Jesus Name. Amen.

Result: A measure of God's life is sent through your spirit to focus on your soul, in particular your mind. This makes you concentrate, meditate and think on the things of God and not the vain, carnal things of this world.

Scripture: Psalm 119:40 "Behold, I have longed after thy precepts, quicken me in thy righteousness."

Prayer: Father, I have longed after Thy precepts, so give life to me in Thy righteousness in Jesus Name. Amen.

Result: A measure of God's life flows from God through your spirit to focus on your mind and body, to give you the wisdom and ability to do the will of God.

Scripture: Psalm 119:88 "Quicken (give life to) me after thy lovingkindness, so shall I keep the testimony of thy mouth".

Prayer: Father, give life to me according to Thy lovingkindness, so shall I keep the testimony of Thy mouth in Jesus Name. Amen.

Result: A measure of God's life flows from God through your spirit to focus on your soul and body bringing to you the necessary wisdom and ability to do the will of God.

Scripture: Psalm 119:107 "I am afflicted very much, quicken me according to thy word."

Prayer: Father, give life to me according to Thy Word, so that I will not be afflicted very much in Jesus Name. Amen.

Result: A measure of God's life and power is sent through your spirit into your soul, body and surroundings, shielding you from Satanic forces, thus making the afflictions that come against you light and not heavy.

Scripture: Psalm 119:149 "Hear my voice according unto thy lovingkindness: O Lord, quicken me according to thy judgement."

Prayer: Father, hear my voice according unto Thy lovingkindness, give life to me according to Thy judgement in Jesus Name. Amen.

Result: A measure of God's life is sent to your human spirit

Scripture:	Psalm 119:154 "Plead my cause and deliver me, quicken me according to thy word."
Prayer:	Lord, plead my cause and deliver me, give life to me according to Thy word in Jesus Name. Amen.
Result:	A measure of God's life, enough to enable you overcome any danger you are facing consciously and unconsciously is sent to your spirit and from there to your soul, body and circumstances as the need arises.
Scripture:	Psalm 119:156 "Great are your tender mercies, O Lord, quicken me according to thy judgements."
Prayer:	Father, great are Your tender mercies O Lord, give life to me according to Thy judgements in Jesus Name. Amen.
Result:	A measure of God's life, based on His mercy and how much life you have given to others, is deposited into your human spirit by the Holy Spirit.
Scripture:	Psalm 119:159 "Consider how I love thy precepts: quicken me, O Lord according to thy lovingkindness in Jesus Name.
Prayer:	Father, consider how I love Thy precepts, give life to me according to Thy lovingkindness in Jesus Name. Amen.
Result:	A measure of God's life, based on the grace of God and how well you have used the life that has been given to you previously to purify your soul (mind, will and emotions) is deposited into your spirit by the Holy Spirit.

Scripture:	Psalm 143:11 "Quicken me, O Lord, for Thy name's sake for Thy righteousness' sake bring my soul out of trouble."
Prayer:	Heavenly Father, give life to me for Your name's sake and for Your righteousness' sake bring my soul out of trouble in Jesus Name. Amen.
Result:	A measure of God's life is sent into your spirit and soul making you more Christ like.
Scripture:	John 3:36 "He that believeth on the Son hath everlasting life…"
Confession:	I believe on the Son, the Lord Jesus Christ, and I have everlasting life now, in Jesus Name. Amen.
Result:	A measure of God's life is sent to your spirit from Christ by the Holy Spirit.
Scripture:	John 6:47-48 "Verily, verily I say unto you, he that believeth on me hath everlasting life, I am that bread of life."
Confession:	I believe on the Bread of life, the Lord Jesus, I have everlasting life now, in Jesus Name. Amen.
Result:	A measure of God's life is sent into your body through your spirit by the Holy Spirit. That life, now present in your body, begins to do a cleansing work ridding your flesh of sin, causing it to become holy and sanctified.

*

Scripture: Romans 8:10-11 "And if Christ be in you, the body is dead because of sin, but the spirit is (has) life because of righteousness. But if the Spirit that raised up Jesus from dead dwell in you, He that raised up Christ from the dead shall also quicken your mortal bodies by His Spirit that dwelleth in you".

Prayer: Christ is in me, my spirit has life now because I am righteous: in rightstanding with God. Father, by Your Spirit Who lives in me, give life now to my physical member in a measure that is more than enough, to keep me in divine healing and health, to cause my youth to be renewed like the eagle's, and to flush out of (by reversing in) my soul and body all of the sin nature, sicknesses, diseases, impurities, infirmities and so every effect of the law of sin and death operating therein, in Jesus' name.

Result: A measure of God's life first sent to your spirit by the Holy Spirit, then from your spirit by the power of the Holy Spirit, this life injected into your physical body, washing it clean from sin thus spiritual death. (Eph.5: 26; Heb. 10: 22).

*Scripture: I Thessalonians 3:12 "And the Lord make you to increase and abound in love one toward another, and toward all men, even as we [do] toward you."

Prayer: Father, make us to increase and abound in compassion: spiritual sensitivity to be touched with God's feelings for the needs, weaknesses and sufferings of the lost, the oppressed, the sick, the ignorant, the weak and the specific people I will be praying for even as You do toward them in Jesus' Name.

31

Result:	A measure of God's life is sent to your spirit by the Holy Spirit to your soul to have compassion and to be sensitive to the needs, and infirmities of others, especially those whom you are praying for, enabling you to pray for them as Jesus would.
*Scripture:	I John 2:14b "… I have written unto you young men, because ye are strong, and the Word of God abideth in you, and ye have overcome the wicked one."
Confession:	I am strong and I have overcome the wicked one, Satan himself in Jesus Name.
Result:	A measure of God's strength is sent from the Holy Spirit into your spirit causing the word of God in your spirit to be "pumped" out with enough force to overcome all enticements and weaknesses Satan has been instilling in your soul and body.
*Scripture:	I John 4:4 "Ye are of God little children, and have overcome them: because greater is He that is in you than he that is in the world."
Confession:	Because greater is He that is in me than he that is in the world, I have overcome all evil spirits in Jesus Name. Amen.
*Scripture:	John 7:37-38 "…If any man thirst, let him come unto me and drink. He that believeth on me, as the scripture hath said, out of his belly shall flow rivers of living water."

Prayer: Father, fill me afresh with the power of the Holy Spirit in the inner man and so cause to flow out of our spirits rivers of living water, as I go into prayer now, in Jesus Name.

Result: Your spirit is filled afresh with the power of the Holy Spirit and by that power, rivers of living water will flow out of your spirit to meet your needs in prayer and the needs of men as you minister to them. Of course, your spirit must be full of living water before such water can be pumped, so to speak, by the power of the Spirit of God. One can think of having the power of the Spirit as having an electric pump which pumps water at a high speed and pressure out of a well. This can be compared to drawing water out of a well with just a rope and bucket. That is what it is like when we minister without the power of the Holy Spirit; the power of God comes out of us in very little measures, and so we do not see great results. We fill the well, our human spirit with water (the life of God), by praying and confessing words of life.

It is useful to memorize these scriptures, so that one can use them in prayer to draw life and power from God anytime, anywhere. This memorization can be effected by the constant use of these prayers and confessions. Over a period of time of constant use, they will remain permanently imprinted upon our minds. The results also become manifest over a period of time and not always immediately.

Note:
The scriptures asterisked are the High Activity Life and Power Scriptures. They are useful for replenishing the human spirit, soul and body with the life and power of God, after a period of concentrated prayer. Also, they can be used to replenish the heart to make powerful confessions and prayers when time does not permit the use of all the life and power scriptures. Note however, that it is always best to use ALL the life and power scriptures for concentrated prayer (see Chapter 5) as a habit.

The Holy Spirit and Prayer

2

THE BAPTISM OF THE HOLY SPIRIT

A reality we can and should experience, because we are in Christ, is the baptism with the Holy Spirit.

Acts 1: 5
For John truly baptized with water, but ye shall be baptized with the Holy Ghost not many days hence.

The word 'baptize' means "to immerse completely in." For instance a tumbler immersed in a bucket of water is not only full of water, but is surrounded entirely by water. Water is a type of the Spirit of God. To be baptised in the Holy Spirit means to be immersed in the person of the Holy Spirit, so that His power fills and surrounds you completely.

Every born again Christian has the Holy Spirit (Romans 8:9). However, not every born again Christian is baptized with the Holy Spirit. Returning to our tumbler/water illustration, a tumbler can contain some water (may be half or one third full), but the tumbler is not baptized in water.

However, every born again Christian has the right to, can and should be baptized in the Holy Spirit.

FUNCTIONAL IMPORTANCE OF THE HOLY SPIRIT BAPTISM

Functionally, a person baptized in the Holy Spirit can have the Spirit of God manifest Himself through that person in an unlimited degree. This can be seen in John 7:37-39. The scripture says for a person baptized in the Holy Ghost;

... Out of his belly shall flow rivers of living water.

"Rivers" speak of an unlimited volume of water. However, for the person who is born again but not baptized in the Holy Spirit, the scripture says in

John 4:14.
The water that I shall give him shall be in him a well of water springing up into everlasting life.

The volume of water obtainable from a well is limited. Thus for a Christian not baptized in the Holy Spirit, the degree to which the Spirit of God can manifest Himself through that Christian is limited.

Therefore, to be able to serve God with an unlimited amount of God's power one needs to be baptized in the Holy Spirit. This was true even for the Lord Jesus Christ (John 3:34; 1:32-33 and Acts 10:38).
This can be seen in John 7:37-39:

If any man thirst let him come unto me and drink. He that believeth on me, as the scripture hath said, out of his belly shall flow rivers of living water. (But this spake he of the Spirit, which they that believe on him should receive: for the Holy Ghost was not yet given, because that Jesus was not yet glorified).

SPEAKING IN OTHER TONGUES: THE LIMIT BREAKER

When a person is baptized with the Holy Spirit, he or she receives the ability to speak in other tongues, unknown to his or her natural mind. In Acts 2:4 we read:

And they were all filled with the Holy Ghost and began to speak with other tongues, as the Spirit gave them utterance.

It is this ability that causes the Holy Spirit to manifest Himself through the individual in an unlimited manner. Before the baptism of the Holy Spirit, a person's prayer life and thus the degree of the manifestation of God's power in his or her life was limited to the understanding of the natural mind, which is ignorant of spiritual realities (1 Corinthians 2: 9-16).

However, with the ability to speak out as the Spirit gives utterance, the Holy Spirit is not hindered or limited by the limited, finite understanding of the natural mind in the things of God. Thus, speaking in tongues makes us break through from the limited to unlimited manifestations of God's power by the Holy Spirit.

BAPTISM AND INFILLING OF THE HOLY GHOST

When anybody gets baptized in the Holy Spirit, at that point in time, the person is also filled with the power of the Spirit. However, this power, is used up as the person gets involved in spiritual activity. It is therefore necessary to constantly receive a fresh infilling of the Spirit through prayer and fellowship with the Lord. We are commanded to be continually filled with the Spirit in

Ephesians 5:18:
And be not drunk with wine, wherein is excess, but be filled with the Spirit...

This implies it is possible not to be. It is possible to be baptized in the Spirit and still be dry on the inside. Just like you can have a sealed tumbler, empty on the inside but immersed in a bucket of water. The tumbler will become full only if the seal on it is removed. We are continually filled with the Spirit as we open up to God constantly in faith and fellowship with Him in prayer.

Thus, after the initial baptism in the Spirit we must thereafter continually be filled with the Spirit by fellowshipping with God in prayer.

HOW TO PRAY FOR THE BAPTISM OF THE HOLY SPIRIT
To be baptized in the Holy Spirit there are certain things a person must do.

(a)   The Person Must Be a Born Again Christian
Only a born again Christian can be baptized in the Spirit. This is stated in John 14:17; (See also Acts 19:2; Luke 11:13).

John 14:17
Even the Spirit of truth, whom the world cannot receive: because it seeth him not, neither knoweth him, but ye know him for he dwelleth with you, and shall be in you.

(b)   Ask God in Faith for the Baptism of the Holy Spirit
Luke 11:13

If ye then, being evil know how to give good gifts to your children: how much more shall your heavenly Father give the Holy Spirit to them that ask him.

A typical prayer would be, "Dear Heavenly Father, I am your child for I have received eternal life, having confessed that Jesus has been raised from the dead and is my Lord and Savior. I therefore come to you to receive the baptism of the Holy Spirit. I believe you now to cause your Spirit to fall on me and fill me. I believe you are doing it now as I ask and I thank you for it in, Jesus Name."

(c) Receive the Holy Spirit by Faith

It is one thing for God to give to us; it is another thing for us to receive from God what He gives. So, we must consciously and deliberately receive the given Holy Spirit by faith. So we can confess that we receive the baptism and infilling of the Spirit in Jesus Name. Optionally, you can open your mouth wide and 'drink' of the Spirit as an act of faith.

Psalm 81:10.
I am the Lord thy God, which brought thee out of the land of Egypt: open thy mouth wide, and I will fill it.

God will honour it.

(d) Speak in other Tongues by faith

After (not before) you have been filled with the Spirit, you can now speak in other tongues.

Acts 2:4
And they were filled with the Holy Ghost and began to speak with other tongues as the Spirit gave them utterance.

You raise your voice, by faith, to vocalize the utterance of the Holy Spirit. What you say will seem foolish to your mind but do it by faith: remember God will not give you a bad gift.

Luke 11:11-13

If a son asks for bread from any father among you, will he give him a serpent instead of a fish? Or if he asks for an egg, will he offer him a scorpion?
If you then being evil, know how to give good gifts to your children, how much more will your heavenly Father give the Holy Spirit to those who ask him! (NKJV)

Raising your voice in faith is like opening a tap: even though there is water in the pipe connected to a tap, if the tap is closed the water will not come out. If your mouth is closed the utterance of the Holy Spirit will not come out even though you have been filled with the power of the Holy Spirit when you asked God to fill you.

Psalms 81:10:

Open your mouth wide, and I will fill it. (NKJV)

In my personal experience it seemed as if I was making up the words myself and just repeating the same words. It sounded so foolish I almost stopped it! But then I remembered what I had heard taught that you do it by faith, so I just continued by faith though it sounded so foolish.

1 Corinthians 2:14

But the natural man does not receive the things of the Spirit of God, for they are foolishness to him; nor can he know them, because they are spiritually discerned. (NKJV)

A few days later a roommate of mine who was not born again told me I was speaking in Aramaic: he was half-Indian, half-Jewish.

I would have missed God's blessing if I had not continued in faith though it sounded foolish and unreal. So you must speak in tongues by faith, by raising your voice and speaking whatever utterance the Holy Spirit gives you after asking for the baptism of the Holy Spirit in faith.

Notice that the people were filled first and then they spoke in tongues as the Spirit gave them utterance, but it was the people that did the speaking. The Holy Spirit will not speak for you or make you speak; you must do the speaking, He will give the utterance.

Again, to speak therefore, simply give audible vocal expression to the activity of the Spirit of God in your heart. What you speak will not make sense to your intellect.

1 Corinthians 14:14
For if I pray in an unknown tongue, my spirit prayeth, but my understanding is unfruitful.

This is normal and to be expected. Just go ahead and keep speaking in faith. Do not be bothered whether the words are well defined or not, just speak on in faith, the fluency of your unknown tongue(s) will increase with time as you pray regularly in tongues (or in the Spirit)!

PRAYING IN THE SPIRIT
This means praying in a supernatural language and utterance given by the unction of the Holy Spirit. It is also known as praying in tongues. When we pray in the Spirit, it is actually the Lord Jesus who is praying for us, through us, as we speak or pray in tongues in utterance given to us by the Holy Spirit.

John 16:13:
Howbeit when he, the Spirit of truth, is come, he will guide you into all truth: for he shall not speak of himself; but whatsoever he shall hear, that shall he speak: and he will show you things to come.

Acts 2:4:
And they were all filled with the Holy Ghost, and began to speak with other tongues, as the Spirit gave them utterance.

Romans 8:26:
Likewise the Spirit also helpeth our infirmities: for we know not what we should pray for as we ought: but the Spirit himself maketh intercession for us with groanings which cannot be uttered.

The high priestly ministry of Jesus Christ for us is released through the supernatural utterance of the Holy Spirit when we pray in tongues.

Hebrews 7:25:
Wherefore he is able also to save them to the uttermost that come unto God by him, seeing he ever liveth to make intercession for them.

There are different modes of praying in the Spirit, each one accomplishing a specific objective, (please see chapter 5 in this book that deals with daily, weekly and monthly prayer for the Christian where these different modes are identified and explained).

However, all praying in the Spirit achieves two things:
(i) It builds you up, charging and strengthening your spirit man. What happens is that the Word of God we have imbibed through meditation in God's Word is, as it were, 'digested' and its power is distributed throughout the spiritman to build up and strengthen him. Further, the spiritman, during the building up prayer in the Spirit, exercises, as it were his spiritual "muscles" so that he will be strong and in good spiritual shape, ready and able to do whatever work he may have to tackle. This is similar to what happens when the physical body eats food (equivalent to meditating in God's Word).

Matthew 4:4
But he answered and said, it is written, man shall not live by bread alone, but by every word that proceedeth out of the mouth of God.

Physical food is digested and the power in the food is distributed to different parts of the physical body to strengthen and build it up, so that the person will remain in good physical shape, ready and able to perform any physical feat he faces. It is possible to eat good food and not exercise. This will not be enough to make us strong. On the other hand if we do not eat well but exercise, our bodies will grow weak and sick. Similarly, we need both to meditate in God's Word and pray in the Spirit in order for our spirits to grow properly and be strong. We see this in Acts 20: 32, I Corinthians 14:4 and Jude 1:20:

Acts 20:32
And now brethren, I commend you to God, and to the word of his grace, which is able to build you up, and to give you an inheritance among all them which are sanctified.

43

1 Corinthians 14:4
He that speaketh in an unknown tongue edifieth (builds up) himself: but he that prophesieth edifieth the church.

Jude 1:20:
But ye, beloved, building up yourselves on your most holy faith, praying in the Holy Ghost.

(ii) Praying in the Spirit also causes you to receive revelation knowledge of the hidden truth of God's Word, both for your personal life and for the treasures of wisdom and knowledge. As you pray in the Spirit with a background of balanced bible reading, these truths are revealed to you by the Holy Spirit.

What happens is that we tap into God's infinite wisdom and knowledge that is potentially in our hearts by the Holy Spirit. As we pray in the Spirit, we are speaking of mysteries, or secrets of God's wisdom:

1 Corinthians 14:2:
For he that speaketh in an unknown tongue speaketh not unto men, but unto God, for no man understandeth him: howbeit in the Spirit, he speaketh mysteries.

This wisdom is a hidden wisdom, hidden not from us, but for us from the devil.
1 Corinthians 2:7-16
But we speak the wisdom of God in a mystery even the hidden wisdom which God ordained before the world unto our glory: which none of the princes of this world knew: for had they known it, they would not have crucified the Lord of glory. But as it is written, eye hath not seen neither ear heard, neither have entered into the heart of man the things which God hath prepared for them that love him. But God hath revealed them unto us by his spirit, for the Spirit searcheth all things yea the deep things of God.

For what man knoweth the things of a man, save the spirit of man which is in him? Even so the things of God knoweth no man but the Spirit of God. Now we have received, not the spirit of this world, but the Spirit which is of God: that we might know the things that are freely given to us of God. Which things also we speak, not in the words which man's wisdom teacheth, but which the Holy Ghost teacheth comparing spiritual things to spiritual. But the natural man receiveth not the things of the Spirit of God for they are foolishness unto him, neither can he know them, because they are spiritually discerned. But he that is spiritual judgeth all things, yet he himself is judged of no man. For who hath known the mind of the Lord that he may instruct him? But we have the mind of Christ.

This wisdom is hidden from the natural mind. As we therefore pray in the Spirit, the secrets we are speaking are unknown to our minds. We see this in

1 Corinthians 14:14.
For if I pray in an [unknown] tongue, my spirit prayeth, but my understanding is unfruitful. (KJV)

The way the Holy Spirit reveals these secrets is as follows:
When you speak in tongues the words you speak paint pictures. For instance if you say 'dog' you have a picture of a dog in your mind: you don't think D-O-G; you think and understand in pictures. So even when you speak in tongues your words are releasing pictures in the spirit realm even though your natural mind does not understand what you are saying. Now some part of these pictures are flashed into your mind by the Holy Spirit, illuminating your understanding using scripture. This is what is known as revelation (Ephesians 1:17-18).

45

1 Corinthians 2:9-10
But as it is written, Eye hath not seen, nor ear heard, neither have entered into the heart of man, the things which God hath prepared for them that love him. But God hath revealed them unto us by his Spirit: for the Spirit searcheth all things, yea, the deep things of God.

It is important to know, however, that you will only get revelation knowledge to the degree to which you know the Word of God. Therefore, consistent, daily reading of the bible is a necessary habit to receive revelation knowledge through the avenue of praying in the Spirit.
The more faithfully you read and understand the scriptures and the more you speak in tongues, or, pray in the Spirit, the more the Holy Spirit can decode and reveal hidden truths for your personal life and for the treasures of wisdom and knowledge to you. The Holy Spirit will also confirm this revelation in your heart through scriptures revealed by independent prophetic and apostolic revelation through teaching, prophecy or visions and dreams and as well as by corresponding supernatural, physical circumstances.

Another advantage of speaking in tongues is that doing so establishes your faith in the physical reality of God's presence, because tongues is the supernatural, physical evidence of the presence of the invisible God. In the same way the sound we hear from the radio is the physical evidence of the presence of the invisible radio waves, tongues is an affirmation of the indwelling presence of the invisible God.

Furthermore, speaking in tongues will help to tame your tongue and so control your whole body and ultimately perfect your conduct (James 3: 2) because when you pray in tongues it is the Lord Jesus who is praying through you by the Holy Spirit, for you to overcome the weaknesses of your flesh (Hebrews 4:14-16; 7:25; Romans 8:26-27; John 16:13).

HOW TO PRAY IN THE SPIRIT
This is discussed in full detail in this book in chapter 5 on Daily, Weekly and Monthly Prayer for the Christian.

How to Pray for Prosperity And to Overcome Sickness And Demonic Oppression

3

INTRODUCTION

There are specific promises and statements in the word of God through which we can draw life and power to overcome sickness and demonic oppression. This chapter outlines what prayers we can make on the basis of these scriptures and how to use these prayers to overcome sickness and demonic oppression.

WHAT TO DO WHEN OPPRESSED BY EVIL SPIRITS

Demons cannot possess the spirit of a born-again Christian, but they can oppress his soul (i.e. mind, will and emotions) and body. This oppression could either be internal or external.

HOW TO KNOW WHETHER OPPRESSION IS INTERNAL OR EXTERNAL

If one has not sinned but still senses demonic influence around one's soul and body, the oppression is external. If one has sinned and senses or perceives demonic influence in one's soul and body, the oppression is internal. You deal with either internal or external demonic oppression in the following ways:

(a)   Internal
(i)   Locate your sin. Repent, confess and get cleansed of it in the following way:

1 John 1:9

If we confess our sins he is faithful and just to forgive us our sins and to cleanse us from all unrighteousness.

Then pray to your High Priest and Advocate, Jesus Christ saying:

"Lord Jesus, I confess the sin (or sins) of …. (mention each sin by name). I repent of it and ask You to forgive and to cleanse me from all the unrighteousness this sin has caused in my heart by Your precious blood. Thank You, Lord."

Further, you say,
"Lord, thank You that in forgiving and cleansing me from this sin, my conscience is purged from this dead work of (mention the sin or sins by name) to serve You, the Living God, because the Word says in Hebrews 9:14:
"How much more shall the blood of Christ… purge your conscience from dead works to serve the living God."

(ii) Fill your spirit with the life and power of God using the high activity life and power scriptures and prayers outlined below:
These high activity scriptures are: John 10:10, Ephesians 3:16-17, Colossians 1:11, John 10:27-28, Isaiah 40:31, Romans 8:10-11, 1Thessalonians 3:12; 1John 2:14; 1John 4:4; 1 John 5:12 and John 7:37-38 in this sequence.

(Please note that it is important and beneficial to pray from the life scriptures in the recommended sequence above).

(iii) Having replenished your spirit with the high activity life and power scriptures, now begin to pray in tongues for about five minutes.

As you do this, say to yourself in your heart thoughts like: "I bind and cast out this spirit of (whatever the oppression is by the effect it is having upon you) in Jesus Name.

HEALING SCRIPTURES

Scripture: Psalm 107:20 "He sent his word and healed them and delivered them from their destructions."

Confession: God sent His Word, the Lord Jesus and healed me in Him (He healed me legally when He bore my sicknesses on the cross, and vitally when He was raised from the dead). The healing power that was wrought in Christ then is still in Him now and I am in Him now. By faith in this Word, I draw on that healing power into my body causing a healing and a cure from any weakness and disease therein in Jesus Name. Amen.

I uproot this spirit from my soul, body or circumstances, in Jesus Name. I love
Righteousness and hate wickedness. I take righteousness, peace and joy (the kingdom of God, Romans 14:17) by faith in Jesus Name. Amen.

(b)   External
1.   Do step (ii) in internal above
2.   Do step (iii) in internal above

WHAT TO DO WHEN SICK
1.   First locate the cause of the sickness. The cause could be natural (e.g. carelessness: exposing one's body to mosquitoes, cold, eating dirty food etc.) or the cause could be spiritual, sin, or, lack of diligence in prayer (which is a sin because **he that knoweth to do good and doeth it not, to him it is sin (James 4:17).** If it is sin, repent and confess it and so get cleansed of it (see step (i) on internal deliverance

50

After this, break the influence of evil spirits that may have been oppressing your soul or body (evil spirits can influence a Christian's body or soul but not his spirit; see internal deliverance above). If it is natural, then go to the next step.

2. Do step (ii) under internal oppression above.

3. Do step (iii) under internal oppression above.

4. Fill your spirit and body with God's life and healing power using all the scriptures at the end of Chapter 1 and the healing scriptures below.

5. Rest for a few hours.

6. Repeat steps 2-5 until your healing fully manifests.

Pray fervently in the Spirit for a short while (10-15 seconds) to release mercy and grace to bring to pass what you have just confessed.

Result: A measure of the healing power flows from your spirit into your physical body, bringing physical healing to your body.

Scripture: Isaiah 53:4-5 "Surely he hath borne our griefs (sicknesses) and carried our sorrows (pains and diseases); yet we did esteem him stricken, smitten of God and afflicted. But he was wounded for our transgressions, he was bruised for our iniquities, the chastisement of our peace was upon him, and with his stripes we are healed."

Confession:	Surely Christ bore my sicknesses and carried my pains, setting me legally free from sickness and pain. When He was raised from the dead, those sicknesses and pains were removed from Him. I am raised now together with Him and so I draw now on that power in Him that removed my sicknesses and diseases from Him. I cause that healing power to flow from the top of my head to the soles of my feet, bringing me healing from all diseases, sicknesses and pains in Jesus Name.
	Pray fervently in tongues for a short while (10-15 seconds) to release mercy and grace to bring to pass what you have just confessed.
Result:	A measure of the healing power flows from your spirit into your physical body, bringing physical healing to your body.
Scripture:	Jeremiah 33:6 "Behold, I will bring it health and cure, and I will cure them, and will reveal unto them the abundance of peace and truth."
Confession:	Father, thank You for the health and cure You have brought me in Christ when You raised Him from the dead. The power that was wrought in Him when He was raised from the dead has cured me and is revealing to me the abundance of peace and truth. I draw on that power now by faith in this word, and cause it to flow into my physical body bringing healing and strength. I draw light from that power into my soul revealing unto me peace and truth in Jesus Name. Amen.

Pray fervently in tongues for a short while (10-15 seconds) to release mercy and grace to bring to pass what you have just confessed.

Result: A measure of God's healing power flows into your body and a measure of God's peace and light flows into your mind.

Scripture: Matthew 8:16-17 "…and he cast out the spirits with his word and healed all that were sick, that it might be fulfilled which was spoken by Isaiah the prophet, saying, Himself took our infirmities and bore our sicknesses."

Confession: Himself, the Word, the living Word, took my infirmities and bare my sicknesses setting me legally free from sickness and disease. When He was raised from the dead, I was vitally set free from sickness and disease. I am free now. I draw on that healing power that was wrought in Him when He was raised from the dead, now I cause that power to flow into my physical body bringing health and healing, in Jesus Name. Amen.

Pray fervently in tongues for a short while (10-15 seconds) to release mercy and grace to bring to pass what you have just confessed.

Result: A measure of God's healing power flows into your physical body now, bringing health and healing.

Scripture: Romans 8:11 "But if the Spirit of him that raised up Jesus from the dead dwell in you, he that raised up Christ from the dead shall also quicken your mortal

Prayer: Father, give life now to my physical members by Your Spirit who lives in me. Let the life bring health and healing to my members now in Jesus Name.

Pray fervently in tongues for a short while (10-15 seconds) to release mercy and grace to bring to pass what you have just confessed.

Result: A measure of God's life flows into your physical members bringing health and healing.

Scripture: 1 Peter 2:24 "Who his own self bare our sins in his own body on the tree, that we, being dead to sins, should live unto righteousness, by whose stripes ye were healed."

Confession: Christ bore my sins and sicknesses on the cross, setting me legally free from sin and sickness. I am dead to sin and sickness and alive unto righteousness and health. When He was raised from the dead, I was healed. I am healed now. The power that healed me when He was raised from the dead is still in Him today. I am in Him today. I draw on that healing power by faith in this word and cause it to flow into my physical members bringing healing and health in Jesus Name.

Pray fervently in tongues for a short while (10-15 seconds) to release mercy and grace to bring to pass what you have just confessed.

Result:	A measure of God's life flows into your physical members bringing health and healing.
Scripture:	1 Peter 2:24 "Who his own self bare our sins in his own body on the tree, that we, being dead to sins, should live unto righteousness, by whose stripes ye were healed."
Confession:	Christ bore my sins and sicknesses on the cross, setting me legally free from sin and sickness. I am dead to sin and sickness and alive unto righteousness and health. When He was raised from the dead, I was healed. I am healed now. The power that healed me when He was raised from the dead is still in Him today. I am in Him today. I draw on that healing power by faith in this word and cause it to flow into my physical members bringing healing and health in Jesus Name.
	Pray fervently in tongues for a short while (10-15 seconds) to release mercy and grace to bring to pass what you have just confessed.
Result:	A measure of God's healing power flows into your physical members bringing you healing and health.

SCRIPTURES AND PRAYERS FOR PROSPERITY

In order for God to prosper you financially and materially, you must honour God with your material substance by being a tither and a giver. The following explanations and prayers show what tithing is and what prayers to make as you tithe and give regularly to get God's blessings in your life.

WHAT IS A TITHE AND HOW DO WE TITHE?

To tithe is to give to God one-tenth (10%) of the material or financial resources that come to us from our labour, or simply by God's favour to us. This giving is to be done as regularly as the resources come in. For example, if you earn a regular salary, you should give one-tenth of it to God as regularly as you get it.

If you are in business, you should give one-tenth of all your profits to God as regularly as you make them. If by God's favour, money or some other source of finances comes to you, you should give one-tenth of such blessings to God as they come in.

The process of giving this money to God is called tithing. The tithe is the money. Tithing is a form of prayer of worship in which we formally give the tithe to God and worship Him. This type of worship of God with one's tithe is one that has always been practiced by men who were in covenant with God. Tithing was practiced by Abraham before the law. We see this in

Genesis 14:18-20:
And Melchizedek king of Salem brought forth bread and wine, and he was the priest of the most high God. And he blessed him, and said, blessed be Abram of the most high God, possessor of heaven and earth: And blessed be the most high God which hath delivered thine enemies into thy hand. And he gave him tithes of all.

Hebrews 7:4
Now consider how great this man was, unto whom even the patriarch Abraham gave the tenth of the spoils.

It was practiced by Israel under the Law of Moses (Hebrews 7:5; Deuteronomy 26:1-15). It is still to be practiced by us under the New Covenant in Jesus Christ today as stated in

Hebrews 7:8
And here men that die receive tithes, but there he receiveth them, of whom it is witnessed that he liveth.

We can draw out a New Testament pattern of tithing by studying the Old Testament type and making appropriate modifications. We do this by studying the Old Testament tithing ceremony illustrated in Deuteronomy 26:1-15 (please look up this scripture now and leave your bible open there so you can follow how the New Testament pattern about to be described comes out of the Old Testament type).

Under the New Covenant, we could do our tithing as follows:
We bring our money or cheque or whatever else we are tithing to God. We should do this alone or where necessary (as it is with a husband and wife) in a small group, privately, in any place where we will not be disturbed. We can put the money on any convenient thing (table, chair, floor etc). We then say the following:

"Lord Jesus, You are my High Priest and I have come to You to worship God our Father with my tithe. I confess I am now in the kingdom of God. I was a sinner, Satan was my father and master and he laid upon me hard bondage and evil entreated and afflicted me. But I cried unto the Lord God my Father in the Name of Jesus, and He delivered me from the kingdom of darkness into the kingdom of His Son, Jesus Christ. Today, God is my Father and I am in the kingdom of Jesus Christ; a land that flows with milk and honey. Now Lord, I have brought the first fruit of the blessings that have come to me, because I am now in Your kingdom. I worship You, Lord with this. I rejoice in every good thing You have given me and my household. Thank You For Your blessings.

Lord, I have been obedient to You and I have brought my tithe to worship You I have given also to the poor and needy out of my substance. I have obeyed Your commandments, I have not forgotten nor transgressed them. Therefore Father, look down from Your holy habitation in heaven and bless me, Your son/daughter in the kingdom of Jesus Christ."

After this, please open your bible to
Malachi 3:10-12
Bring ye all the tithes into the storehouse, that there may be meat in mine house, and prove me now herewith, saith the Lord of hosts, if I will not open you the windows of heaven, and pour you out a blessing, that there shall not be room enough to receive it. And I will rebuke the devourer for your sakes, and he shall not destroy the fruits of your ground, neither shall your vine cast her fruit before the time in the field, saith the Lord of hosts. And all nations shall call you blessed: for ye shall be a delightsome land, saith the Lord of hosts.

Now, make the following confessions.
"Father, I have brought my tithes into Your storehouse (Church or Ministry from where God is feeding you His Word), that there may be meat in Your house. Lord, according to Your Word, open the windows of heaven and empty out upon me blessings I cannot contain. I am proving You with this according to Your Word."

"Satan, you devourer, I rebuke you for my sake in Jesus' Name. You (Satan) shall not destroy any of my possessions, neither shall you interfere with the blessings God is sending to me now. They will come in due season. All nations call me blessed and I am a source of blessing and a delight to humanity in Jesus' Name. Amen."

This ends the tithing. It is good to actually practice this worship of God with our tithe regularly, because it will ascertain the blessings of God upon our finances and keep the devil out of our affairs.

WHAT TO DO IN THE TIME OF NEED
If you have a financial or material need or desire some material thing, first checkup that you have been tithing and giving. If not, do so immediately, with whatever you have, no matter how small.

Secondly, check your motivation and God's will concerning that particular thing. If you believe it is not God's will at that time, forget it. If you believe it is His will, pray and believe you receive the need when you pray (Mark 11:24).

Command the devil to take his hands off your affairs. If you are walking in the Spirit and in the will of God concerning that particular need at that particular time, what you need will come in good time. Learn to fulfill God's conditions and leave the rest to Him. Do not continue to think or fret about the matter. When it comes to mind, thank God for it and forget it. It is not God's will that we set our minds on material things (Colossians 3:2). Concentrate rather on pleasing God, walking in the Spirit, righteousness, peace and joy in the Holy Spirit and the desires of your heart shall come into manifestation. (Psalms 37: 4; Matthew 6: 33 and Romans 14: 17).

TYPICAL SCRIPTURES AND CONFESSIONS FOR PROSPERITY
Scripture: Luke 6:38 "Give and it shall be given unto you, good measure, pressed down and shaken together, and running over, shall men give into your bosom. For with the same measure that ye mete withal it shall be measured to you again."

Confession:	I have given in good measure and cheerfully of my substance, therefore God is causing to come to me favour with men, wisdom and ability so that I will have an abundance of material and financial possessions, so that I can give even more in future in Jesus Name.
	Pray fervently in tongues for a short while (10-15 seconds) to release mercy and grace to bring to pass what you have just confessed.
Result:	God will cause favour, wisdom and ability to enter your soul, body and circumstances causing you to prosper greatly in all you set your hand unto.
Scripture:	2 Corinthians 9:10-11 "Now he that ministereth seed to the sower both minister bread for your food and multiply your seed sown and increase the fruits of your righteousness. Being enriched in everything to all bountifulness, which causeth through us thanksgiving to God."
Confession:	Father, thank You for causing prosperity to come to me, giving bread for my food. Thank You also for multiplying my seed sown. I am enriched in all things to all bountifulness in Jesus' Name.
	Pray fervently in tongues for a short while (10-15 seconds) to release mercy and grace to bring to pass what you have just confessed.

Result: God's wisdom and ability will flow into your soul and body, causing you to prosper in all you do. God's favour will flow into your circumstances, causing you to have favour with men, causing all that is connected with you to prosper. The prosperity that thus comes will cause you to be enriched in all things to all generosity.

Pauline Prayers and Characteristics of Divine Love

4

There are certain prayers recorded in the New Testament which Paul, the Apostle, prayed for the different churches in the New Testament.

We call these prayers the Pauline Prayers, since they were prayed by Paul. The overall essence of these prayers is to:

a)   Give us a perfect knowledge of who we are, what we have and what we can do in Christ.

b)   Perfect us in love.

c)   Ascertain the mercy and grace of God upon us, so that we fulfill perfectly God's plan for our lives on the earth.

We should pray these Pauline Prayers for others and ourselves during the course of our daily prayer life (see Chapter Five on Practical Guidelines to Daily, Weekly and Monthly Prayer for the Christian).

Scripture: Ephesians 1:17-20 "That the God of our Lord Jesus Christ, the Father of glory, may give unto you the spirit of wisdom and revelation in the knowledge of him. The eyes of your understanding being enlightened; that ye may know what is the hope of his calling, and what the riches of the glory of his inheritance in the saints. And what is the exceeding greatness of His power to us ward who believe, according to the working of his mighty power, which he wrought in Christ when he raised him from the dead, and set him at his own right hand in the heavenly places."

Prayer: Dear Father, I pray that You give unto me the spirit of wisdom and revelation in the present, complete knowledge of You so that the eyes of my understanding may be further enlightened, that I may know better, the hope of Your calling upon my life, the riches of the glory of Your inheritance in me as a saint and the exceeding greatness of Your power which You wrought in Christ Jesus when You raised him from the dead in Jesus Name. Amen.

Result: A measure of God's light is sent to your spirit and soul to illuminate your understanding of His calling upon your life, the riches of the glory of His inheritance in you and the exceeding greatness of His power towards you.

Scripture: Ephesians 3:16-19: "That He (God) would grant you, according to the riches of His glory, to be strengthened with might by His Spirit, in the inner man. That Christ may dwell in your hearts by faith; that ye being rooted and grounded in love, may be able to comprehend with all saints what is the breadth, and length, and depth, height; and to know the love of Christ, which passeth knowledge, that ye might be filled with all the fullness of God."

Prayer: Father, we pray that you grant us according to the riches of Your glory to be more strengthened with might by Your Spirit in the inner man so that Christ would dwell more in your hearts by faith; that we become more rooted and grounded in love, that we may be able to comprehend more with all saints what is the breadth, and length, and depth, and the height of the body of Christ; and so to know the love of Christ, which surpaasses knowledge, that we might be filled with all the fullness of God in Jesus Name.

Result: A measure of God's power is sent into your spirit to strengthen your spirit to be able to draw life constantly from Christ, so that the life of God will constantly flow in your soul, causing you to be rooted and grounded in love.

Scripture: Philippians 1:9 "And this I pray that your love may abound yet more and more in knowledge and in all judgement."

Prayer: Father, I pray that my love may abound yet more and more in present, complete knowledge, in all judgement in all things in Jesus Name. Amen.

Result: A measure of God's wisdom flows into your heart giving you the wisdom it takes to walk in love whatever circumstances you may face.

Scripture: Colossians 1:9 "...To desire that ye might be filled with the knowledge of his will in all wisdom and spiritual understanding..."

Prayer: Dear Father, I pray that You fill me with the present, complete knowledge of Your will in all wisdom and spiritual understanding concerning walking in faith and love for and by Your life in Jesus Name. Amen.

what is the breadth, and length, and depth, and the height of the body of Christ; and so to know the love of Christ, which surpaasses knowledge, that we might be filled with all the fullness of God in Jesus Name.

Result: A measure of God's power is sent into your spirit to strengthen your spirit to be able to draw life constantly from Christ, so that the life of God will constantly flow in your soul, causing you to be rooted and grounded in love.

Scripture: Philippians 1:9 "And this I pray that your love may abound yet more and more in knowledge and in all judgement."

Prayer: Father, make me to increase and abound in compassion: spiritual sensitivity to be touched with God's feelings for the needs, weaknesses and sufferings of the lost, the oppressed, the sick, the ignorant, the weak and the specific people I will be praying for even as You do toward them in Jesus' Name.

Result: A measure of God's compassion is sent to your emotions by the Holy Spirit.

Scripture: 2 Thessalonians 3:5 "And the Lord direct your hearts into the love of God, and into the patient waiting for Christ."

Prayer: Father, direct my heart into Your love and into the patience of Christ in Jesus Name. Amen.

Result:	A measure of God's compassion and patience is sent into your heart to enable you to walk in love.
Scripture:	2 Thessalonians 1:11-12 "Wherefore, also we pray always for you, that our God would count you worthy of this calling, and fulfill all the good pleasure of his goodness, and the work of faith with power. That the name of our Lord Jesus Christ may be glorified in you, and ye in him, according to the grace of our God and the Lord Jesus Christ."
Prayer:	Heavenly Father, I pray that You will vouchsafe and count me worthy of this high calling to which You have called me in Christ and fulfill all the good pleasure of Your goodness and the work of faith with power in and through me, so that the Name of my Lord Jesus Christ may be glorified in me and I in Him, according to and by Your mercy Father, the grace of our Lord Jesus Christ and the help of the Holy Spirit in Jesus Name. Amen.
Result: life is	This prayer will ascertain that God's plan for your fulfilled in spite of your human weaknesses.

CONFESSIONS, MEDITATIONS AND PRAYERS TO WALK IN LOVE ACCORDING TO 1 CORINTHIANS 13:4-8

Lord, have mercy on us so we receive Your Blood to cleanse us from ALL unrighteousness (Heb. 8:12; 1Jn.1:7).

In Jesus name we have life (visualize the flow of life into you as living water Jn. 4:10, 14).

Lord have mercy on us as we pray (Rom.9.16, Heb.4.16, Jude.1.20-21)

I am patient and kind in all things, I am forbearing and longsuffering, I am not jealous or envious. I rejoice at the blessing of others. I am not boastful, I boast and glory only of Jesus Christ because God gave me all I have (1 Cor.13:4a).

Meditate: Think for a short while on what you have just said with a determination to practice it.

Pray in tongues for a short while as above and as you pray, say in your heart and determine to practice what you have just confessed, mentally

acknowledging with thanksgiving (Col.4:2) the presence of the three Persons of the God-Head in the air around you (Psalms 16:8).

Time: About 1 minute.

Lord, have mercy on us so we receive Your Blood to cleanse us from ALL unrighteousness (Heb.8:12; 1Jn.1:7), Your life (Jude 1:21) and power (Acts 1:8) in sufficient measure for this prayer:

I am not proud (1 Cor.13:4b); I am courteous to all men and treat them with respect either big or small, or rich or poor. I am always polite and not rude to others (1 Cor.13:5a).

Meditate: Think for a short while on what you have just said with a determination to practice it.

Pray in tongues for a short while as above and as you pray, say in your heart and determine to practice what you have just confessed, mentally acknowledging with thanksgiving (Col.4:2) the presence of the three Persons of the God-Head in the air around you (Psalms 16:8).

Time: About 1 minute.

Lord, have mercy on us so we receive Your Blood to cleanse us from ALL unrighteousness (Heb.8:12; 1Jn.1:7), Your life (Jude 1:21) and power (Acts 1:8) in sufficient measure for this prayer:

I do good to all men including myself (Matt.22:39) but I am not selfish so I seek the good of others (Phil.2:4) also. I do not insist on my own rights or my own way except when it concerns the vital will of God and even then with meekness and reverence (1Pt.3:15; 1 Cor.13:5b).

Meditate: Think for a short while on what you have just said with a determination to practice it.
Pray in tongues for a short while as above and as you pray, say in your heart and determine to practice what you have just confessed, mentally acknowledging with thanksgiving (Col.4:2) the presence of the three Persons of the God-Head in the air around you (Psalms 16:8).
Time: About 1 minute.

Lord, have mercy on us so we receive Your Blood to cleanse us from ALL unrighteousness (Heb.8:12; 1Jn.1:7), Your life (Jude 1:21) and power (Acts 1:8) in sufficient measure for this prayer:

I forgive people from the heart (Matt.18:35) when they wrong me or anytime I see them sin by instantly asking God in my thinking for mercy to cleanse their sins by the blood of Jesus (Heb.8:12; 1Jn.1:7), receive life for them (Jude 1:21; 1Jn.5:16) and later pray for them in tongues (1Cor.14:4; Eph.4:16); relating to them in wisdom but without bitterness (Eph.4:31) but with goodwill (Rom.13:10).

Meditate: Think for a short while on what you have just said with a determination to practice it.

Pray in tongues for a short while as above and as you pray, say in your heart and determine to practice what you have just confessed, mentally acknowledging with thanksgiving (Col.4:2) the presence of the three Persons of the God-Head in the air around you (Psalms 16:8).

Time: About 1 minute.

Lord, have mercy on us so we receive Your Blood to cleanse us from ALL unrighteousness (Heb.8:12; 1Jn.1:7), Your life (Jude 1:21) and power (Acts 1:8) in sufficient measure for this prayer:

I do not worry (Matt.6:25-32). I cast all my cares and burdens on Jesus (1Pt.5:7) by prayer, supplication and thanksgiving with my thoughts (Phil.4:6-7). I love righteousness and hate sin and wickedness (Heb.1:9) abstaining from all appearances of evil (1The.5:22). I do not rejoice when others go wrong, rather, I pray for them (1 Cor.13:6). I am always ready to believe the best of others. I never give up on them even when they are wrong. I keep praying for them (1 Cor.13:7).

Meditate: Think for a short while on what you have just said with a determination to practice it.

Pray in tongues for a short while as above and as you pray, say in your heart and determine to practice what you have just confessed, mentally acknowledging with thanksgiving (Col.4:2) the presence of the three Persons of the God-Head in the air around you (Psalms 16:8).

Time: About 1 minute.

Total Time: 5 minutes daily.

69

You should do this as the first thing every day before you say other prayers and read your bible because these prayers (to walk in the fear and love of God) position you to be able to receive from God answers to all other prayers. (See our minibook "Daily Guide to Keeping Yourself in the Love of God and Balanced Bible Reading" for more details).

Practical Guidelines to Daily, Weekly and Monthly Prayer for the Christian   **5**

Prayer is the key to victorious Christian living when it is done properly. When Jesus prayed, He did not   pray haphazardly, but He used the principles of the law of the Spirit of life in Christ Jesus (Romans 8: 2).

The scripture says of Jesus, 'in the days of his flesh when he had offered up prayers and supplications with strong crying and tears' (Hebrews 5: 7). The scripture also tells us we should pray always with all types of prayer in the Spirit (Ephesians 6: 18). This is how Jesus prayed every day, not just at Gethsemane, and if we want to have an equally successful prayer life we must pray the same way.

We do not attempt here to do an exposition on these principles but it suffices to say that they have solid scriptural support and have been found to work in practice. Furthermore, it is as you put them into practice and study the scriptures concerning them that you will understand them more fully. However, one can immediately put them into practice by following the practical guidelines given below.

The guidelines are not a formula, or a set of rules that must be rigidly adhered to. They are to set a pattern and a standard that we should seek to attain. However, there is room for flexibility by the Spirit of God to make adjustments to suit the particular circumstances and the level of spiritual development of each individual.

You should do this as the first thing every day before you say other prayers and read your bible because these prayers (to walk in the fear and love of God) position you to be able to receive from God answers to all other prayers. (See our minibook "Daily Guide to Keeping Yourself in the Love of God and Balanced Bible Reading" for more details).

Consequently, for prayer to be effective, there needs to be a background of spiritual warfare in which this satanic opposition is overcome.

When we come to pray, therefore, we use the weapons of our warfare: the blood of Jesus (Revelation12: 11), the Word of God (Hebrews 4: 12), and the power of the Holy Spirit (John 7: 37 - 39; Zechariah 4: 12).

In the natural, when soldiers fight, they use guns and there are three things you do with a gun - you clean it, you load it with bullets and you fire it in the right direction to kill your enemy. Spiritually, we do the same things; we clean our hearts with the blood of Jesus, we load our hearts with the Word of God and we fire by the power of the Holy Spirit to kill our enemy, the satanic nature in the flesh and in the air (Ephesians 2: 2).

CLEANSING WITH THE BLOOD
We must begin by cleansing with the blood, which is done by confessing our sins (1John.1: 9). When we confess our sins, the blood of Jesus goes into operation to cleanse and to remove any impediment or block of sin that would otherwise hinder the free, full flow of God's life and power into our spirits.

Sin acts as a blockage to the flow of God's life from God into our spirits just like food remnants and oil block the flow of water in a kitchen sink from flowing out through the drainpipe. The blood of Jesus is like the plunger or chemical reagent that removes the blockage so that the water can flow freely out of the sink.

LOADING WITH THE WORD

Then we proceed to fill our spirits with the life of God using the Word of God (Hebrews 4:12; Ephesians 6:17). The life of God is the spiritual liquid inside God that makes God 'God'. The bible calls it 'living water.' That is the simplest way to think about it. So we fill our spirits with this living water, using the promises from the Word that promise us this life, or, living water (see chapter 1).

When we pray from each of these promises in faith, a measure of this living water flows into our spirits and gradually, our spirits are filled with living water. The bible says, 'with the increase of our lips shall we be filled' (like you fill the tank of a car with petrol; Proverbs18: 20).

(John 1:16)
And of his fullness have all we received, and grace for grace.
This refers to the measure upon measure of the living water that we receive as we pray sequentially from scripture after scripture to fill our spirits with the life of God.

As a part of loading with the Word, we must also pray according to the Word and the will of God (1John 5:14; Jeremiah 1:12) by finding some basis in the scriptures that support what we are praying for. For example, the bible says:

Philippians 4:19
But my God shall supply all your need according to his riches in glory by Christ Jesus.

We must, therefore, make sure that whatever we pray is in line with the Word of God so that God can have a legal basis upon which to answer our prayer request (Psalms 115:16; Numbers 23:19; Psalms 138:2;
Jeremiah 1:12).

73

FIRING BY THE SPIRIT

After loading with the Word we now proceed to fire by the Spirit. When we fire by the Spirit, we are praying in a supernatural utterance given by the Holy Spirit with different types of prayer, like Jesus prayed, with prayers (or petitions), supplications, strong crying (groaning, intercessions and travail) and thanksgiving (1Timothy 2:1).

WHEN SHOULD WE PRAY?

The Bible tells us in 1 Thessalonians 5: 17 to pray without ceasing. Now, since prayer basically is communication or fellowship with God, it follows that it is possible to pray without ceasing by being in communion with God 24 hours a day.

However, since one lives in this world, there are other things one has to do, therefore, it is not possible to have concentrated prayer 24 hours a day. Even Jesus did not. He had seasons of concentrated prayer, which he consciously concluded at some point in time:
Luke 11:1
And it came to pass, that, as he was praying in a certain place, when he ceased, one of his disciples said unto him, Lord, teach us to pray,

However, as explained above, He was in constant communion with God, and so He did pray without ceasing. When we therefore talk about times of prayer, we talk about times of deliberate, conscious, concentrated communion with God. For successful Christian living, it is necessary to have such sessions of prayer daily.

Probably the most important time one should pray is in the morning. If we have victory over Satan in the morning, we are almost certain to have victory throughout the day. If on the other hand, we do not pray effectively in the morning, it is unlikely the rest of the day will be victorious spiritually.

MORNING PRAYER

Ideally, one should try to get out of bed and start praying by 5am. The morning session of prayer should last between 1½-2 hours including both individual and corporate or family prayers.

Start your praying by praying for about 10-15 minutes to keep yourself in the love of God everyday (see page 8 of our mini book: Daily Guide for Keeping Yourself in the Love of God and Balanced Bible Reading, by Olubi Johnson).

This should be done first before praying with all types of prayer, and should be done even on days when you wake up late and there is no time to pray with all types of prayer, since walking in the love of God positions you to receive from God answers to all your other prayers (1John 3:22-23).

Prayer For Spiritual Victory: Using All Types of Prayer in the Spirit *** for About One Hour

Step 1: Cleansing of Sins (1John 1:9; Hebrews 9:14) (1 minute)*

We begin by saying:

Father, I confess our (self, immediate, household etc.) sins (e.g. prayerlessness, disobedience, spiritual slothfulness, intemperance, waywardness of mouth, lack of patience and love, lying, lack of diligence in prayer, sexual immorality in thought, word and deed, covetousness, idolatry, pride, stubbornness, rebellion, envy, unforgiveness, dishonesty, worry and unbelief) and the sins of our people, fathers & forefathers of greed, murder and wickedness. I receive for all of us forgiveness, cleansing and the purging of our consciences from these dead works and a guilty conscience to serve You the living God according to Your word that says, "If we confess our sins, He is faithful and just to forgive us our sins, and to cleanse us from all unrighteousness (1Jn.1:9)", and, "How much more shall the blood of Christ purge your conscience from dead works and a guilty conscience (Heb.10:22) to serve the living God (Heb.9:14)"; and, "Whosoever sins you remit they are remitted unto them (Jn.20:23)." I forsake (Pro.28:13) these sins and break their yokes by practicing the Word by the mercies (Rom. 12:1) of God with a continually increasing determination (Pro.24:16) and giving all diligence (2Pet.1:5- 10) to stop sinning and so to receive more mercies to triumph (Rom.9:16) over the judgement for these sins (Jas.2:13) and their effects (2Sam.21:1,3).

Step 2: Receive Mercy, Grace and Help (Romans 9:15; 2 Corinthians 12:9; Romans 8:26) (2 minutes)*

We pray and say:
In Jesus' Name we have life.
Father, I repent of my sins and determine to do all you reveal to me. Holy Spirit, please help me to enjoy communion and fellowship with You so my prayers will be refreshing, exciting and will avail much. Help me to find the yoke easy and the burden light and to redeem the time as I pray. In this regard, Lord Jesus, Heavenly Father, please release Your grace and mercy upon me. I receive these things by faith now and thank You, in Jesus' Name.

[It is vital to acknowledge (mentally) the Holy Spirit as a Person in this way so your prayer will not be mechanical but refreshing].

*** See Appendix 1
Step 3: Receive Life and Power from God using the Life and Power Scriptures (2 Pet. 1:4; Pr. 8:20,21) and make your prayer request in the understanding (Jn. 16:23; Num. 23:19) (10 minutes)*

Step 3a: Life and Power scriptures (please refer to chapter 1 to do this)
Step 3b: Making your prayer request.

We pray and say:
In Jesus' Name we have life.
Father give life to our spirits now and that in a measure that is more than enough to enable me to pray effectually and fervently for spiritual victory in the lives of myself, members of my immediate family and household today in the following manner: in tongues and with groanings by the Holy Spirit with all kinds of prayer to generate and to release more than enough of the life and power of God to cause us this day:-

(a)   to be divinely protected and preserved from all spiritual and physical evil and attack, both human and demonic and from spiritual and physical sickness and death (Psalm 91: 15)

(b) to will and do of God's good pleasure (Philippians 2:13), so that today, we will

-Walk worthy of the Lord unto all pleasing (Colossians 1:10).
-be fruitful in every good work (Colossians 1:10) and
-Become more conformed to the image of Christ (Romans 8:29), in Jesus' Name.

Step 4:   Prayer in the Spirit with all types of prayer (1 Timothy 2:1-4;   Ephesians   6:18; Hebrews 5:7)   (35-40 minutes.)*

We pray and say:

In Jesus name we have life.

Holy Spirit, please pour afresh on me the spirit of grace, travail and compassion enabling me to pray with all types of prayer in the Spirit as I pray now. Dear Lord Jesus, in this regard, please release your grace; Father, please release Your mercies as I pray now in Jesus' name. (It is vital to acknowledge the Holy Spirit as a Person in this way so your prayer will not be dull and mechanical, but refreshing.)

Proceed to pray with all types of prayer in the Spirit, which are:

PETITION: We begin with petition; talking to God in a supernatural language (tongues) concerning the intricacies and details of our prayer request. We do not know these details, but the Holy Spirit knows them and He helps us to articulate them properly. For one hour of prayer we spend about 4-5* minutes in this mode, as led by the Spirit.

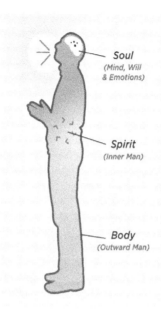

Soul
(Mind, Will
& Emotions)

Spirit
(Inner Man)

Body
(Outward Man)

Https://www.spcconline3.net/2019/10/prayer-illustrations-petition/

SUPPLICATION: We then switch into another mode of prayer called supplication, during which we are asking God for mercy to deal with the infirmities of our flesh that would otherwise hinder our effective praying. The process of supplication involves praying in tongues and groaning alternately. When we pray in tongues, we are asking God for mercy for specific infirmities known to the Holy Spirit, but unknown to us (Ps.19:12), and then when we groan, we are releasing some of the living water we filled our spirits with. From our belly it flows up into our souls and down into our flesh to deal with those specific infirmities of our flesh. By praying in this way, we pull down strongholds in our minds; we cast down imaginations; we bring our thoughts into captivity to the obedience of Christ; keeping our attitudes meek and lowly and crucifying the flesh so that we can pray effectively.

We spend another 4-5* minutes in this mode, as led by the Spirit, for one hour of prayer.

Soul
(Mind, Will & Emotions)

Spirit
(Inner Man)

Body
(Outward Man)

https://www.spcconline3.net/2019/10/prayer-illustrations-supplication/

TRAVAILS, GROANINGS OR INTERCESSIONS: We then change into yet another mode of prayer in the Spirit, which is groanings, or travail, or intercessions. These are different expressions for the same thing and during groanings, or travail, or intercessions, what we are doing is releasing the power of God from our bellies to go into the air, to overcome the satanic opposition in the air and to fill the air with the power of God to create and bring (or birth) into physical manifestation the answer to our prayer. It is called travail because it is very similar to what a woman experiences when she is having a baby: we contract our stomach muscles and groan as we do so.

The bible says 'Out of his belly shall flow rivers of living water' (John 7:37-38). So we pray with travail, or, intercessions, or, groanings in this way for about 20-22 minutes*, as led by the Spirit, for one hour of prayer.

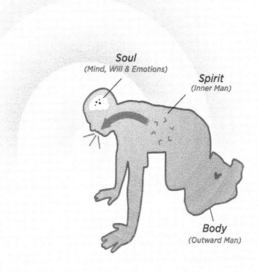

https://www.spcconline3.net/2019/10/prayer-illustrations-groanings/

SUPPLICATION: Then we go into another round of supplication, just like the first one, but here now we are dealing specifically with the infirmities of the people through whom the answer will come. We spend another 4-5 minutes* in this mode, as led by the Spirit, for one hour of prayer.

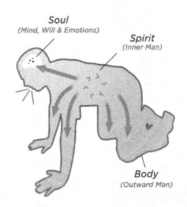

Soul
(Mind, Will & Emotions)

Spirit
(Inner Man)

Body
(Outward Man)

https://www.spcconline3.net/2019/10/prayer-illustrations-supplication/

SILENCE: Next, we have a time of silence. Prayer is communing with God. It is not a monologue but a dialogue. We must, therefore, give God a chance to speak to us when we are not talking. During this time of silence we think on the Word of God and we think about what we have been praying about, and God is able to speak to us through our thoughts (note: His speaking to us in this way is not limited to the time of silence). We spend about 2-3 minutes as led by the Spirit, giving God a chance to speak to us.

THANKSGIVING AND WORSHIP: After the time of silence, we then go into a time of thanksgiving and worship in the Spirit. Again, we begin to give thanks to God in a supernatural language given by the Holy Spirit, to thank Him for all the great things He has done during our prayer in the spirit. We do not know them in detail, but the Holy Spirit does and therefore helps us to give thanks well.

82

This time of thanksgiving is also a time of power because the bible says, God 'inhabits the praises of Israel' (Ps.22:3) and 'Abraham was strong in faith; giving glory to God.' (Rom.4:20). During this time we may also worship and praise God as the Spirit leads us. Spend 4-5 minutes* in this mode as led by the Spirit for one hour of prayer.

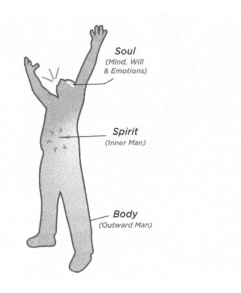

Step 5: Binding the Devil (Matthew 12:29) (1min)*At the end of all the praying in the Spirit, we replenish our hearts with the life of God using just the high activity life and power scriptures (see chapter 1). This is like refilling the tank of a car with petrol after a long journey.

Then pray and say:
In Jesus' Name we have life.
Father, give life to our spirits now and that in a measure that is more than enough to bind the devil, loose the angels, confess the word and pray in the Spirit concerning this prayer request in Jesus Name. Amen.

In Jesus' Name we have life.
Wicked spirits in the heavenlies and in the earth that I have overcome during this time of prayer, I destroy your works, resist and bind you in Jesus' Name. Amen.

In Jesus Name we have life.
Evil spirits in the earth that may be oppressing or attacking the souls, bodies and circumstances of ourselves (self, members of my immediate family and household) and the specific people I have prayed for, I cast you out, destroy your works, resist and bind you in Jesus' Name. Amen.

Step 6: Loosing the Angels in the Understanding (Matthew 18:18) (1 minute)*

Pray and say:
In Jesus Name we have life.
I loose the angels of God with the seven spirits of God: the spirit of the fear of God, of knowledge, understanding, wisdom and revelation, counsel, might and the spirit of love to go forth now in the name of Jesus to occupy the air and so enforce and execute God's perfect will concerning my prayers in Jesus Name. Amen.

Step 7: Confession of Faith to bring the answer into Physical Manifestation (Mark 11:23; Romans 10:10) (1min)*

Pray and say:
In Jesus Name we have life.
God's perfect will concerning my prayers is established and in full physical manifestation in Jesus' Name. Amen.

In Jesus Name we have life.

All the people and groups of people God is using to answer my prayers have the mind and ability of Christ, are meek and lowly in heart, redeeming the time and are temperate and protected from death in this regard in Jesus' name.

**Total time of Prayer: About one hour (Matthew 26:40; Acts 3:1)

*These timings (Ecclesiastes. 3:1) are a standard that have been found by practice (Acts 1:1; Ezra 7:10) to maximize the efficacy of a prayer unit of one hour. However, you are free to vary the timing but only as led by the Holy Spirit (1 Corinthians. 14:15,32). If you are unable to pray for the specified time, do your best and trust God's grace to help you to improve with practice.

SELF JUDGEMENT

Do this self-judgement to clean with the blood daily.

"Father, I confess our (i.e. self, immediate family, household, etc) sins, so clean with the blood from ALL unrighteousness" (to cover the multitude of sins, 1Pet. 4: 7-8, keep the commandment without spot, 1Tim. 6: 14: and edify ourselves in love, Eph. 4: 15; 1Jn. 5: 16); visualize the sprinkling of the blood of Jesus on your navel (symbolic of your connection to God) to remove all spots, blocks or clots).

In Jesus name we have life (visualize the flow of life into you as living water Jn. 4:10, 14).

Lord have mercy on us as we pray (Rom.9.16, Heb.4.16, Jude.1.20-21)

I judge myself (1Cor.11:31) and condemn my wicked actions and attitudes of omission and commission hitherto. I receive mercy unto eternal life (Jude 21) to soften my heart to enable me to repent and be faithful (1 Cor.7:25); receiving wisdom and instruction and have victory and triumph over judgement (Jas.2:13, 2Cor.2:14) in Jesus' Name. Amen.

SETTING YOUR WILL

Do this setting of will at least once weekly.

In Jesus Name we have life.
I John 2: 14: *We are strong and have overcome the wicked one, Satan himself.*

In Jesus Name we have life.
I John 4: 4: *We have overcome all evil spirits, because greater is He that is in us than he that is in the world.*

In Jesus Name we have life.
Matthew 18: 18: Evil spirits who may be oppressing or attacking the souls, bodies and circumstances of ourselves, members of our immediate families and households, I cast you out, destroy your works, resist and bind you in Jesus Name. Amen.

Lord, have mercy on us so we receive Your Blood to cleanse us from ALL unrighteousness (Heb. 8:12; 1Jn.1:7), Your life (Jude.1:21) and power (Acts 1:8) in sufficient measure for this prayer:

I set my will and determine to apply completely and operate diligently (Psalms 119: 112) the principles of perfection doing all God reveals to me to do (Phil.2:13): inquiring of

and acknowledging the Lord in my thinking by frequently (at least once every conscious hour (Matt.24:42)) and at every opportunity and during temptations asking the Holy Spirit with thanksgiving (Col.4:2) for mercy unto eternal life to be faithful to do all things with love (1Cor.16:14); and also by watchful praying in tongues to wash feet (Jn.13:14): forgive, confess and cleanse our sins by the blood of Jesus (Jn.20:23; 1Jn.1:9); ask for life (1Jn.5:16) and pray in tongues (Jude 20-21; 1Cor.14:18) for us to bind the devil (Mt.11:12; Mt.12:29) in the air (Eph.2:2), enforce the kingdom: righteousness, peace and joy in the Holy Spirit (Rom.14:17) during temptations; so praying without ceasing (in my heart) in all honesty and humility, without fear, boldly and diligently by the mercy and grace of God.

Pray fervently in tongues for a short while (10-15 seconds) to release mercy and grace to bring to pass all you have just confessed. Meditate (think on and say in your heart) the confession as you pray in tongues.

*See appendices 2 and 3 for details

Lord, have mercy on us so we receive Your Blood to cleanse us from ALL unrighteousness (Heb. 8:12; 1Jn.1:7), Your life (Jude.1:21) and power (Acts 1:8) in sufficient measure for this prayer:

I submit my will firstly to God through His word, and also through my conscience with reverence (without God I cannot survive spiritually: John 1: 1). Secondly, I submit to those in authority over me (spiritual fathers and mothers, pastors, husband, parents, boss, etc) with reverence (without them I cannot survive physically and progress spiritually: Eph. 6: 1-3) and thirdly, to those I am in authority over (flock, wife, children, servants, etc.) with meekness (without them I cannot progress spiritually or physically: Eph. 4:16) when what they say is in line with the Word of God and will of God, but is inconvenient for my pride and feelings, making me lower (Phil.2:7) than I think or know I am. I esteem my colleagues as better than myself and maintain an attitude of reverence to those above and meekness to those below me in authority, as well as towards all men, even when I think or know I am right and they are wrong.

Pray fervently in tongues for a short while (10-15 seconds) to release mercy and grace to bring to pass all you have just confessed. Meditate (think on and say in your heart) the confession as you pray in tongues.

WASHING OF FEET AND BINDING THE DEVIL

After the morning prayer with all types of prayer in the Spirit has been completed you now 'wash feet' and bind the devil by praying as shown below:

Lord, have mercy on us so we receive Your Blood to cleanse us from ALL unrighteousness (Heb. 8:12; 1Jn.1:7), Your life (Jude.1:21) and power (Acts 1:8) in sufficient measure for this prayer:

We love God with all our hearts: wills, minds, emotions and strength (Matt.22:37); and we love our brethren as Christ loves them (Jn.13:34): washing our feet (Jn.13:14-15) by forgiving, confessing and so cleansing our sins by the blood of Jesus (Jn.20:23; 1Jn.1:9), asking life for us (1Jn.5:16) and praying for us in tongues (1Cor.14:18; Jude 20) to cover for every hour for the six hours from 06.00hrs to 12.00hrs. We also frequently [at least once every conscious hour (Matt. 24:42)] and at every opportunity and during temptations ask

the Holy Spirit with thanksgiving in our thinking (Col.4:2) for mercy unto eternal life (Jude 21) to be faithful (1Cor.7:25), to do all things with love (1 Cor.16:14); by washing feet (Jn.13:14-15): by forgiving, confessing and so cleansing our sins by the blood of Jesus (Jn.20:23; 1Jn.1:9), asking life (1Jn.5:16) for us and praying for us in tongues (Jude 20-21; 1Cor.14:18) to bind the devil (Matt.11:12; 12:29) in the air (Eph.2:2) to enforce the kingdom: take and do righteousness, peace and joy in the Holy Spirit (Rom.14:17), at least once every six hours, at every opportunity and during temptations as led by the Spirit (Gen. 24:27) as we think (Phil.4:8) and act on the word (Phil.4:9) to help us repent to will and do of God's good pleasure (Phil.2:13, Heb. 13:21).

This same process should be repeated to cover for the hours from 1200hrs to 1800hrs and from 1800hrs to 2400hrs and from 2400hrs to 0600hrs as early as possible as you have opportunity during the day, (at least once every 6 hours (2Sam.6:13; Ex.25:10; Deut. 6:7; Mk.13:35)) for a balanced walk in the Spirit.

GENERAL CONFESSIONS
Make the following confessions at least once a week (Gen.1-3- Gen.2:2) Praying in tongues briefly (about 1 minute) after each confession, meditating on (saying in your heart) the confessions as you pray in tongues.

REVELATION AND GIFTS BLOCK
Lord, have mercy on us so we receive Your Blood to cleanse us from ALL unrighteousness (Heb. 8:12; 1Jn.1:7)

In Jesus' Name we have life (visualize the flow of life into you as living water Jn. 4:10, 14).

Lord have mercy on us as we pray (Rom.9.16, Heb.4.16, Jude 1.20-21)

Ephesians 1:17-20: Father, please give us the spirit of wisdom and revelation in the present complete knowledge of You, so the eyes of our understanding may be further enlightened, that we may know better, the hope of Your calling upon our lives, the riches of the glory of Your inheritance in us, and the exceeding greatness of Your resurrection power in Christ towards us as saints in Jesus' Name. Amen.

Lord, have mercy on us so we receive Your Blood to cleanse us from ALL unrighteousness (Heb. 8:12; 1Jn.1:7), Your life (Jude.1:21) and power (Acts 1:8) in sufficient measure for this prayer:

Philippians 1:9: Father, please may our love abound yet more and more in present complete knowledge, in all judgement, in all things in Jesus' Name. Amen.

Lord, have mercy on us so we receive Your Blood to cleanse us from ALL unrighteousness (Heb. 8:12; 1Jn.1:7), Your life (Jude.1:21) and power (Acts 1:8) in sufficient measure for this prayer:

Lord, have mercy on us so we receive Your Blood to cleanse us from ALL unrighteousness (Heb. 8:12; 1Jn.1:7), Your life (Jude.1:21) and power (Acts 1:8) in sufficient measure for this prayer:

*** (Pray this daily)
Ephesians 3:16-19: Father, we pray that you grant us according to the riches of Your glory to be more strengthened with might by Your Spirit in the inner man so that Christ would dwell more in your hearts by faith; that we become more rooted and grounded in love, that we may be able to comprehend more with all saints what is the breadth, and length, and depth, and the height of the body of Christ; and so to know the love of Christ, which surpaasses knowledge, that we might be filled with all the fullness of God in Jesus Name.

Lord, have mercy on us so we receive Your Blood to cleanse us from ALL unrighteousness (Heb. 8:12; 1Jn.1:7), Your life (Jude.1:21) and power (Acts 1:8) in sufficient measure for this prayer:

2Thessalonians 1: 11-12: Father, please vouchsafe (guarantee) us worthy of the high calling You have called us to in Christ (of His perfection and fullness) and fulfil this day in and through us all the good pleasure of Your goodness and the work of faith with power, so the name of the Jesus Christ will be glorified in us and we in Him, according to and by Your mercy, His grace and the help of the Holy Spirit in Jesus' Name. Amen.

Lord, have mercy on us so we receive Your Blood to cleanse us from ALL unrighteousness (Heb. 8:12; 1Jn.1:7), Your life (Jude.1:21) and power (Acts 1:8) in sufficient measure for this prayer:

The gifts of the Spirit (I Cor.12: 7-10): the word of wisdom, word of knowledge, discernings of spirits, gift of special faith, workings of miracles, gifts of healings, prophecy, diverse kinds of tongues and interpretations of tongues are manifest through us as the Holy Spirit wills (1Cor.12:11) as we speak in tongues and lay hands on the sick and oppressed (Mk.16:17-18) and praise and worship God (1Cor.14:15).

MIND BLOCK

Lord, have mercy on us so we receive Your Blood to cleanse us from ALL unrighteousness (Heb. 8:12; 1Jn.1:7), Your life (Jude.1:21) and power (Acts 1:8) in sufficient measure for this prayer:

*** (Pray this daily)

We think only on things that are true, honorable, just, pure, lovely, of good report, of excellence, and of praise (Phil. 4: 8). We bring into captivity every thought to the obedience of Christ (2 Cor. 10:5), and we have the humility and ability of the mind of Christ (1Cor.2:16; Phil.2:5).

Lord, have mercy on us so we receive Your Blood to cleanse us from ALL unrighteousness (Heb. 8:12; 1Jn.1:7), Your life (Jude.1:21) and power (Acts 1:8) in sufficient measure for this prayer:

We acknowledge God frequently (as led by the Spirit (Gen.24:27)) and at every temptation (2Cor.10:5)) with thanksgiving in our thinking for mercy unto eternal life (Jude 21) to be faithful to do all things with love (1Cor.16:14), by praying frequently in tongues (at least once every six hours (2Sam.6:13; Mk.13:35), and at every opportunity (1Cor.14:18) and in every temptation with our thoughts and actions (Jas.1:22; 2:18; 2Cor.10:5; Pro.20:8) to commune and fellowship with God; so He directs our paths (Pro.3:6b) and keeps us in perfect peace (Rev.3:6; Jude 20, 21; Is.26:3; Rom.8:6).

Lord, have mercy on us so we receive Your Blood to cleanse us from ALL unrighteousness (Heb. 8:12; 1Jn.1:7), Your life (Jude.1:21) and power (Acts 1:8) in sufficient measure for this prayer:

We exercise our hearts in righteous practices (Ps.15:2) and our hearts are established in righteousness (Ps.112:8) so that we cannot continue in sin (Pro.28:13a); therefore we have the sure mercies (Pr.28:13b) of David turning our captivities into freedom and restoring all our fortunes (Ps.126:4).

Lord, have mercy on us so we receive Your Blood to cleanse us from ALL unrighteousness (Heb. 8:12; 1Jn.1:7), Your life (Jude.1:21) and power (Acts 1:8) in sufficient measure for this prayer:

** (Pray this daily)
We are slow to speak, swift to hear and slow to wrath (Jas.1:19), we let our words be few (Ecc.5:2), speaking only what God permits (John 8: 26).

Lord, have mercy on us so we receive Your Blood to cleanse us from ALL unrighteousness (Heb. 8:12; 1Jn.1:7), Your life (Jude.1:21) and power (Acts 1:8) in sufficient measure for this prayer:

** (Pray this daily)
Ephesians 5: 16: We redeem the time always, because the days are evil.

CONSISTENCY BLOCK

Lord, have mercy on us so we receive Your Blood to cleanse us from ALL unrighteousness (Heb. 8:12; 1Jn.1:7), Your life (Jude.1:21) and power (Acts 1:8) in sufficient measure for this prayer:

** (Pray this daily)

Father, please strengthen us with all might according unto Your glorious power unto all patience and long-suffering with joyfulness (Col.1:11), so we will be consistently diligent in our prayer lives, walk in the Spirit by the life of God, prompt and diligent obedience to the voice and leadings of the Holy Spirit, bible reading and study (2Tim.2:15; 3:16-17), witnessing by the Spirit and living a fasted life (Is.7:15; Eccl.10:16-17), all daily (Luke 9: 23); and fasting and prayer at least once weekly (Is.58:6-13) in Jesus' Name. Amen.

Lord, have mercy on us so we receive Your Blood to cleanse us from ALL unrighteousness (Heb. 8:12; 1Jn.1:7), Your life (Jude.1:21) and power (Acts 1:8) in sufficient measure for this prayer:

We continue in righteousness (Heb.1:9) applying completely and operating diligently the principles (Jas.1:27a) of perfection in God's presence; feeding the poor and visiting the afflicted (Jas.1:27b), having fullness of joy and pleasures forever more (Ps. 16:11).

Lord, have mercy on us so we receive Your Blood to cleanse us from ALL unrighteousness (Heb. 8:12; 1Jn.1:7), Your life (Jd.1:21) and power (Acts 1:8) in sufficient measure for this prayer:

** (Pray this daily)

We are vessels of honour, sanctified and meet for the Master's use (2Tim.2:20,21), prepared unto every good work, so we abstain from all sexual impurity in thought, word and deed (1Th.5:22); by fulness of joy and pleasures forever more in the presence of God (Ps.16:11). We dress decently and comely to the glory of God (1Cor.10:31). We flee fornication, adultery and any type of sexual impurity because it destroys our physical bodies (1Cor.6:18), dishonours God (1 Cor.6:19-20), and disinherits us of the Spirit without measure.

PHYSICAL AND MATERIAL NEEDS BLOCK

Lord, have mercy on us so we receive Your Blood to cleanse us from ALL unrighteousness (Heb. 8:12; 1Jn.1:7), Your life (Jude.1:21) and power (Acts 1:8) in sufficient measure for this prayer:

Matthew 6: 10: God's perfect will, plan and purpose for Nigeria (or mention your nation by name), Israel, America and all nations is in full physical manifestation.

Lord, have mercy on us so we receive Your Blood to cleanse us from ALL unrighteousness (Heb. 8:12; 1Jn.1:7), Your life (Jude.1:21) and power (Acts 1:8) in sufficient measure for this prayer:

By the stripes of Jesus (1 Peter 2: 24) and His resurrection life and power (Rom.8:11; 2 Cor.4:10-11; 2Cor.5:4), we are healed and live in divine healing and health, so we keep the laws of hygiene (Dt.23:10-14) and natural medicine (Lev.13-15; Is.38:21), of diet (Lev.11) of physical exercise (1 Tim.4:8) and of rest (Gen.2:2-3; Ex.20:8-11).

Lord, have mercy on us so we receive Your Blood to cleanse us from ALL unrighteousness (Heb. 8:12; 1Jn.1:7), Your life (Jude.1:21) and power (Acts 1:8) in sufficient measure for this prayer:

We keep the laws of prosperity: sowing (2Cor.9:6-9) by giving our tithes and offerings (Mal.3:10-12; Gal.6:6; 1Cor.9:8-14) promptly, completely, regularly and cheerfully; watering (Ps.1:3) by praying and walking in the Spirit (Jn.7:38-39; Rom.8:10-16;26) effectually and fervently (Jam.5:16); harvesting by practicing and investing in honest (Tit.3:14) ventures, so we have knowledge, understanding, wisdom (Col.2:3), skill, divine guidance, strength, ability, favour with God and men (Lk.2:52); in all we do. We succeed, excel and prosper (Ps.1:3, Jos.1:8; 3 Jn.2) in all that we do. Our God supplies all of our needs (Phil.4:19). We have a hundred-fold return in this lifetime (Mk. 10:30) on every financial seed we have sown thus far and on everything we have given because of Jesus and the gospel.

Lord, have mercy on us so we receive Your Blood to cleanse us from ALL unrighteousness (Heb. 8:12; 1Jn.1:7), Your life (Jude.1:21) and power (Acts 1:8) in sufficient measure for this prayer:

Psalms 91:1-13: We keep ourselves in the love of God, so no evil shall befall us, neither shall any plague come near our dwelling for God has given His angels charge over us, they keep us in all our ways and protect our spirits, souls and bodies and everything we have from damage, loss, theft and natural disasters.

Lord, have mercy on us so we receive Your Blood to cleanse us from ALL unrighteousness (Heb. 8:12; 1Jn.1:7), Your life (Jude.1:21) and power (Acts 1:8) in sufficient measure for this prayer:

Psalms 91:14-16: We have set our love upon God, so with long life will God satisfy us and show us His salvation even the perfection and fullness of Christ.

Lord, have mercy on us so we receive Your Blood to cleanse us from ALL unrighteousness (Heb. 8:12; 1Jn.1:7), Your life (Jude.1:21) and power (Acts 1:8) in sufficient measure for this prayer:

We are profitable (Lk.17:10) sons (Gal.4:1, Eph.4:14-15), having the spirit of excellence, so we are not satisfied with only doing what we have been commanded to do, but in addition we do that which is pleasing in God's sight (1 Jn.3:22).

MONTHLY PRAYERS

On a monthly basis you need to pray with all types of prayer in the Spirit, as you do for the Morning Prayer, to cover for certain basic needs for your life. This implies spending at least one hour a month (you should do more one-hour units of prayer if you are under attack in a particular area) for each of the following topics:

1. You should pray to go to bed early and wake up early. This may seem like a strange topic, but your entire spiritual life and the lives of your family depend on your morning prayer being prayed REGULARLY, and the devil will try to attack your consistency in this area.

2. If you are married or engaged you need to spend at least one hour a month praying for your spouse or fiancée to be conformed to the image of Christ and to fulfill the purpose of God for his/her life. If you are not married yet you should use this slot to pray for a godly future partner.

3. You should pray at least one hour a month for your children and household. You should pray that the children will grow up to be godly as Christ grew as a child (see Luke 2:52) and to be conformed to the image of Christ. If you do not have children then you should pray that God will give you godly seed and pray for your immediate family and household.

4. Pray for your finances to water and harvest your seed sown. You can include in this praying for your secular job or business.

5. Pray concerning your Christian service in the house of God. If you do not have a function yet in the house of God then pray that God will show you what He wants you to do for Him in His house. Every saint should be working for God at one level or another.

6. Pray for the healing and health of yourself and family so that Satan will not be able to use sickness and disease to hinder or attack you.

7.   Pray for the salvation (i.e to be born again) of members of your extended family (Acts 16:31)
8.   Pray for the nation according to 1Timothy 2:1-2. This should actually be done weekly as referred to in chapter 6 of this book.

Praying for The Nation   **6**

INTRODUCTION AND SCOPE OF PRAYER FOR THE NATION

In 1 Timothy 2:1- 4 we read:
I exhort therefore, that, first of all, supplications, prayers, intercessions, and giving of thanks, be made for all men; for kings, and for all that are in authority; that we may lead a quiet and peaceable life in all godliness and honesty. For this is good and acceptable in the sight of God our Saviour; Who will have all men to be saved, and to come unto the knowledge of the truth.

Here, we are commanded by God to pray for the nation. This should be done consistently by all Christians so that, like it says in verse 2, "We may lead a quiet and peaceable life in all godliness and honesty."

Basically, in praying for the nation, we break the influence of Satan and rulers of the darkness of this world over our nation and leaders and pray that God's Spirit, power and wisdom will influence our people and leaders, so that we as Christians may lead a quiet and peaceable life in all godliness and honesty.

Prayer for the nation will not eradicate completely all the social and economic problems in the nation. In fact, such a complete eradication will only come during the millennial reign of Christ on the earth (Revelation 20:3-4) which takes place after this church dispensation. The job of the church is to preach the gospel of Jesus Christ to all men in all nations (Matthew 24:14). The essence of prayer for the nation is to see to it that an atmosphere of peace and quiet prevails in the nation, so that the church can do the job of preaching the gospel maximally.

Praying for the nation will, therefore, to some degree help solve and overcome the social and economic problems of the land, but it will not and is not designed to eradicate such in this dispensation.
If Satan through the negligence of the church in prayer can create an atmosphere of war and disruption, the gospel will be hindered and many men that should hear the gospel and live would die without hearing it. Thus we see that praying for the nation is of utmost importance in helping the church do the job of preaching the gospel.

We should therefore, endeavor to pray for the nation for at least one hour every week.

HOW TO PRAY FOR THE NATION
1.   Use the format discussed in detail in chapter 5, which deals with praying in the Spirit with all types of prayer for one hour.

When making your petition in the understanding, before proceeding to pray in the Spirit, make petition as follows:

Prayer for the nation will not eradicate completely all the social and economic problems in the nation. In fact, such a complete eradication will only come during the millennial reign of Christ on the earth (Revelation 20:3-4) which takes place after this church dispensation. The job of the church is to preach the gospel of Jesus Christ to all men in all nations (Matthew 24:14). The essence of prayer for the nation is to see to it that an atmosphere of peace and quiet prevails in the nation, so that the church can do the job of preaching the gospel maximally.

Then pray and say:
In Jesus Name we have life.
Father, give life to our spirits now and that in a measure that is more than enough to enable me pray effectually and fervently to bind the devil, loose the angels, confess the Word and pray in the Spirit concerning this prayer request, in Jesus Name. Amen.

In Jesus Name we have life.
Wicked spirits in the heavenlies and in the earth that I have overcome during this time of prayer for the nation, I destroy your works, resist and bind you in Jesus Name. Amen.

In Jesus Name we have life.
Evil spirits in the earth that may be oppressing the souls, bodies and circumstances of ourselves (self, members of immediate family and household) and the specific people I have prayed for, I cast you out, destroy your works, resist and bind you in Jesus Name. Amen.

In Jesus Name we have life.
I loose the angels of God with the seven spirits of God: the spirit of the fear of God, of knowledge, understanding, wisdom and

revelation, counsel, might and the spirit of love to go forth now in the name of Jesus to occupy the air and so to enforce and execute God's perfect will concerning my prayers for the nation in Jesus Name. Amen.

In Jesus Name we have life.
God's perfect will concerning my prayers for the nation is established and in full physical manifestation in Jesus' name. Our leaders in this nation (name the nation) rule and reign righteously and in the fear of God so that we all in this land lead a quiet and peaceable life in all godliness and honesty therein.

In Jesus Name we have life.
All the people and groups of people God is using to answer my prayers for the nation (name the nation) especially, the president, members of the executive, legislature, judiciary, security and armed forces and the Zion church have the mind and ability of Christ, are meek and lowly in heart, redeeming the time and are temperate and protected from death in this regard in Jesus' name. Pray in the Spirit briefly (about 10-15 seconds) concerning these confessions.

Father, I thank You for Your mercy, Lord Jesus, I thank You for Your grace, Holy Spirit, I thank You for Your love and help in Jesus Name. Amen.

Total time of prayer: About one hour (Matthew 26:40; Acts 3:1).

Fasting and Prayer 7

WHAT IS FASTING?

A fast is a period of time of partial or total abstention from eating and other physical activities, in which we seek God in prayer and study and meditation in his word (Daniel 9: 3; 2 Chronicles 20: 3; Acts 13: 2-3).

WHY WE SHOULD FAST

We should fast so as to be able to have periods of time seeking God and His word without interruption and give the whole power of our spirit, soul and body to seeking God. The power of the human spirit is what fuels all physical activities (such as eating, working etc.).

According to Proverbs 4:23:
Keep thy heart with all diligence; for out of it are the issues of life.

When we fast, the power that would have been diverted to performing those activities we abstain from is used in prayer. This makes our prayers more effective and powerful and our hearing or receiving from God more accurate (Proverbs 14:30; James 2:26).

HOW TO FAST

Fasting can be done in two basic ways:
(a) Corporate Fasting
(b) Individual Fasting

(a) Corporate Fasting
Here a fast is proclaimed for a group of believers by those in position of authority or leadership. All the believers then fast and seek God together during the same period of time for the same purpose.

Joel 2:15
Blow the trumpet in Zion, sanctify a fast, and call a solemn assembly.

2 Chronicles 20:3
And Jehoshaphat feared, and set himself to seek the Lord, and proclaimed a fast throughout all Judah.

(b) Individual Fasting
Here a fast is proclaimed by an individual. This is something private between him and God (Daniel 9:3).

We read of this in Matthew 6: 16-18:
Moreover, when ye fast, be not as the hypocrites, of a sad countenance: for they disfigure their faces, that they may appear unto men to fast. Verily I say unto you, they have their reward. But thou, when thou fastest, anoint thine head, and wash thy face; That thou appear not unto men to fast, but unto thy Father which is in secret: and thy Father, which seeth in secret, shall reward thee openly.

GENERAL GUIDELINES TO FASTING
Whether we fast corporately or individually it is good and beneficial to observe the following guidelines:

(a)   Formally proclaim the fast before God and dedicate it to Him. Ask for His strength and help during the fast so that you can complete it successfully (Matthew 6 :18; Isaiah 40: 31).

(b)   Decide the purpose of the fast (i.e. the reward you expect from the fast Matthew 6: 18). There should always be a reason for fasting. It can be some specific desire (e.g. salvation or deliverance, spiritual exercise and fellowship with God). This type should be done regularly (2 Corinthians 11: 27); e.g. Weekly, fortnightly, month etc). The fasts need not be long or total; you can have short, partial fasts.

2 Corinthians 11:27.
In weariness and painfulness, in watchings often, in hunger and thirst, in fastings often, in cold and nakedness.

But you should practice fasting regularly, for the spiritual benefits this exercise in godliness gives you (I Timothy 4:7).

(c)   During the fast, reduce all physical activity to the barest minimum, especially talking and working.

Isaiah 58:3, 13.
Wherefore have we fasted, say they, and thou seest not? Wherefore have we afflicted our soul and thou takest no knowledge? Behold in the day of your fast ye find pleasure, and exact all your labours.
If thou turn away thy foot from the sabbath, from doing thy pleasure on my holy day: and call the sabbath a delight, the holy of the Lord, honourable; and shall honour him, not doing thine own ways, nor finding thine own pleasure, not speaking thine own words…"

Spend time in the Word (reading, studying, meditating) in prayer and worship of God. Alternate between these as led by the Spirit. Remember all prayer is only effective when based on God's Word. The Word of God wielded by the Holy Spirit, is the source of power (Ephesians 6:17-18; Hebrews 4:12).

(d)   Nearly all fasts in the bible include taking water. We abstain from food; but we take water. It is good to take water during a fast as this helps clean out of our bodies any poisons that are released therein as the body seeks nourishment from food it has stored previously.

(e)   Do not fast so long as to become physically unable to even read your bible or pray properly. A general rule is if you are involved in other activities by necessity (e.g. work), never go on a total fast for more than a few (say, three) days. If you are led to go on a long fast (more than three days) go into a "wilderness".

According to Matthew 4: 1-2:
Then was Jesus led up of the spirit into the wilderness to be tempted of the devil. And when he had fasted forty days and forty nights, he was afterward an hungred.

Wilderness means a place where you have no contact with anything and anyone. You then seek God there. It is easier to carry on a long fast under such conditions. However, you should not do anything to injure your body or health, it is not the will of God (3 John 2). Remember a fast can be partial (Daniel 10: 3). Let the Spirit of God lead you and give you wisdom in each situation.

(f)   If you break a fast before you planned to (because of temptation to eat or physical weakness (I John 1:9)) repent and plan better with God next time. You get better in fasting with practice and as you practice, you study your body and circumstances and learn how best to go about it.

(g)   For a private fast, if others get to know that you are fasting, this does not spoil the fast. Sometimes it is necessary to let people know you are fasting so as not to offend them. What can spoil a fast is a hypocritical attitude of wanting people to know you are fasting, so they can have a high spiritual regard for you. This stems from spiritual pride. As much as possible avoid letting other people know either by your conduct or appearance as stated in Matthew 6: 17-18.

THE REWARDS OF FASTING
Isaiah 58 tells us what kind of fast God expects of us and the rewards that come from such fasts.
Briefly they are:

(i)   Increase in revelation knowledge of God's word.

Isaiah 58: 8:
Then shall thy light break forth as the morning and thine health shall spring forth speedily and thy righteousness shall go before thee;   the glory of the Lord shall be thy rereward.

(ii)   Spiritual strength and power to get immediate answers to prayer (Mark 9:14-29).

Isaiah 58:9:
Then shalt thou call, and the Lord shall answer; thou shall cry and   he shall say, here I am. If thou take away from the midst of thee, the   yoke, the putting forth of the finger and speaking vanity;

(iii)   Spiritual growth and maturity to be able to bring forth and build up spiritual children by your life and prayers (Isaiah 66:8; Galatians 4:19).

Isaiah 58:12:

And they that shall be of thee shall build the old waste places: thou shalt raise up the foundations of many generations; and thou shall be called, the repairer of the breach, the restorer of the paths to dwell in.

(iv) Development of the fruit of the Spirit or the divine character in your life

Isaiah 58: 11:

And the Lord shall guide thee continually, and satisfy thy soul in drought, and make fat thy bones and thou shalt be like a watered garden, and like a spring of water, whose waters fail not.

(v) Spiritual power to be able to exercise authority over all the power of darkness including wicked spirits in heavenly places of the earth (Ephesians 6:12).

Isaiah 58: 14:

Then shalt thou delight thyself in the Lord; and I will cause thee to ride upon the high places of the earth and feed thee with the heritage of Jacob thy father: for the mouth of the Lord hath spoken it.

(vi) Material prosperity to be able to have plenty and good food for nourishment and health of your body (Isaiah 58:14).

Psalm 103:5:

Who satisfieth thy mouth with good things: so that thy youth is renewed like the eagle's.

Study the entire Isaiah 58 with the above as a guide.

COMMENTS ON FASTING AND PRAYER

God has revealed to us in the New Testament that He expects us to fast (Matthew 6:16). However, we are not told when and how often to fast. We have however found by practice that it is spiritually beneficial to have one day to fast and pray every week. During this day of fasting, you follow the guidelines given above and find time, (usually a most convenient time is at night, maybe between 9.00pm and 6.00am the next morning) to spend some 3-4 hours in continuous prayer in one hour periods using the life scriptures and prayer in the Spirit to pray for spiritual victory for your life for that week (see step 5 in morning prayer in Chapter 5 for details). We strongly recommend this habit of regular, consistent prayer with fasting. This spiritual exercise keeps you in excellent spiritual shape ensuring that you do not grow weary or negligent in your daily prayer life during that particular week.

Isaiah 40:31:
But they that wait (serve God in fasting and prayer regularly) upon the Lord shall renew their strength; they shall mount up with wings as eagles; they shall run and not be weary; and they shall walk and not faint.

Prayer of Praise and Worship **8**

WHAT IS WORSHIP?

Worship is the art of pleasing and serving God. To worship God is to please and serve Him. We can and should serve and please God in everything we do, so true worship in its entirety is a total lifestyle and not just a period of time of singing and praising God.

HOW TO WORSHIP
In John 4:24, the Lord Jesus said that,
God is a Spirit and they that worship Him must worship him in spirit and in truth.

We are to, yea, must worship God in Spirit and in truth.

WORSHIPPING GOD IN TRUTH
To worship God in truth is to worship Him in sincerity and in reality. It is to worship God with all of our lives (our time, our money, our whole being) and not just with our lips (Mk.7:6-7).

Romans 12:1 says:
I beseech you therefore, brethren, by the mercies of God, that ye present your bodies a living sacrifice, holy, acceptable unto God, which is your reasonable service.

We are told to present our bodies a living sacrifice to God, holy and acceptable, and this is called our reasonable service or worship of God. To worship God in truth is to live a holy life and keep His commandments. To worship God is to walk in the Spirit and to walk in divine love. It is this worshiping God in truth that

WORSHIPPING GOD IN SPIRIT

The Lord Jesus said God is a Spirit. For worship of God to minister effectively to God, that worship must have spiritual substance in it. Under the old covenant, men worshiped God by making physical sacrifices like the killing of bullocks and lambs. Under the new covenant our sacrifices of worship to God are primarily spiritual sacrifices.

1 Peter 2:5:
Ye also, as lively stones, are built up a spiritual house, an holy priesthood to offer up spiritual sacrifices, acceptable to God by Jesus Christ.

These are made in the form of the words we speak and sing to God. Spiritual and physical sacrifices are contrasted in Ps 50:13-14. God is a Spirit and what is going to minister to Him must be spiritual. Our words contain spiritual substance.

John 6:63:
It is the spirit that quickeneth; the flesh profiteth nothing: the words that I speak unto you, they are spirit, and they are life...

During a prayer of praise and worship (be it in the Spirit or in the understanding (1 Corinthians 14:2; 14-16), the words we speak minister glory to God. That glory is a mixture of the light, life and love of God that comes from the Word of God that has been put in our hearts by meditation and prayer (see prayers at end of chapter 1).

SACRIFICE AND QUALITY OF WORSHIP IN THE SPIRIT

True worship in the spirit is a sacrifice. The reason for this is that what we give to God comes out of the deposit of God's word put in our hearts by meditation and prayer. It takes labour in prayer and meditation to put God's word and life in our hearts, as shown in Proverbs 10:16.

The labour of the righteous tendeth to life the fruit of the wicked to sin.

It is out of this labour we give to God spiritual substance in our worship in the spirit. This is just like under the old covenant when a man would labour to get money, and then use some of the money he earns to live to buy a lamb or bullock to sacrifice to God. We labour in the Word and prayer to put God's life in our hearts, we use some of it to live ('for the just shall live by faith' - Galatians 3:11) and some of it we give to God as sacrifice in praise and worship.

When we thus labour in the Word and prayer and therefore live a holy life, the quality of our worship in the spirit will be very high and very pleasing to God. If we are spiritually slothful (see Hebrews 6: 12) and do not labour much in the word and prayer our lifestyle will not please God well and so the quality of our worship will be low. The quality of our worship is then dependent on the state of our hearts whether they are full of God's life and power or not. Let us therefore endeavour to be diligent in prayer and meditation of God's Word so that our worship to God in the spirit can be of a truly high quality. The prayer of praise and worship is the highest form of prayer because it is the only type of prayer in which we give something to God. In all other types of prayer, we get something from God and give nothing to Him.

ACCEPTABLE WORSHIP

All worship to God by His children is acceptable, be they of high or low quality. However, God's will for us is to increase the quality of our worship. Further, God meets us all at our different levels of development; we are to give to God the best we can give at any time and this will be acceptable to and pleasing to Him (Psalm 50:23).

However, if we have unconfessed sin in our hearts, our worship will not be acceptable to God (Psalm 66:17-18). If we confess our sins, He will forgive and cleanse us and our worship will then be acceptable. God does not want us under condemnation with a sin consciousness (see 1John 1:7; Hebrews 10:16-22).

All our worship goes through the Lord Jesus Christ, our High Priest, to God the Father, and so once we have no sin standing between us and Him, all our worship is acceptable to God.

I Peter 2:5
Ye also, as lively stones, are built up a spiritual house, an holy priesthood, to offer up spiritual sacrifice, acceptable to God by Jesus Christ.

GUIDELINES TO WORSHIP IN THE SPIRIT

There are a few guidelines we can use to worship God in the spirit, songs and words that will make our worship of a high quality:

(i)   Create in yourself by faith a consciousness of the reality of God's presence (Hebrews 11:6, 27; 2Corinthians 4:18) and fill your heart with the Life, using Life Scriptures (see chapter 1).

(ii)   Minister praise to God with your understanding with words taken from God's Word that speak of His greatness and goodness (this can be in the form of known choruses and hymns). This is the lowest form of praise.

(iii)   Minister praise to God with your spirit with words in other tongues given by the utterance of the Holy Spirit (see Acts 2:11; Acts 10:46). This could be in the form of songs or just words. This is a higher form of praise.

(iv)   Minister praise to God with your spirit in words known to your mind but which come by prophecy. This form of prophecy is praise wherein one speaks by the inspiration of the Spirit of God's greatness and goodness. An example of this is shown in

1 Chronicles 25:1-3
Moreover David and the captains of the host separated to the service of the sons of Asaph, and of Heman, and of Jeduthun, who should prophesy with harps, with psalteries and with cymbals: and the number of the workmen according to their service was: Of the sons of Asaph; Zachur, and Joseph, and Nethanianh, and Asarelah, the sons of Asaph under the hands of Asaph, which prophesied according to the order of the king. Of Jeduthun: the sons of Jeduthun; Shabiah, and Lattitiah, six, under the hands of their father Jeduthun, who prophesied with a harp, to give thanks and to praise the Lord.

It could be in form of tongues and interpretation of a song or psalm first spoken in other tongues, or, it could be just direct prophecy. This type of prophecy carries with it no prediction at all and so it can be stirred up and practiced.

2 Timothy 1:7
Wherefore I put thee in remembrance that thou stir up the gift of God, which is in thee by the putting on of my hands.

With this kind of prophecy, there is no danger or harm done when a mistake is made. It develops with use and practice. It is this gift of prophecy that Paul speaks about in

1 Corinthians 14:1, 5, 31.
Follow after charity, and desire spiritual gifts, but rather that ye may prophesy.
I would that ye all speak with tongues but rather that ye prophesied; for greater is he that prophesieth than he that speaketh with tongues. Except he interpret, that the church may receive edifying.
For ye may all prophesy one by one, that all may learn, and all may be comforted.

As one uses prophecy in this area of praise and worship, the gift will develop and one can use it proficiently in the area of edification, exhortation and comfort (1 Corinthians 14:3). It is the highest form of praise and worship, since it blesses God and your spirit and soul.

The praise with the understanding blesses God and your soul alone, the praise with the Spirit blesses God and your spirit alone. A lot of the book of Psalms contains this type of prophecy that simply magnifies God, but contains no prediction.

During worship one can start at the lowest level and move up to the highest level of praise. This should be practiced daily in one's private prayer life. Further these same principles can be put into operation in corporate worship, the excellence and beauty of corporate worship comes out when the individuals have learnt to flow with the Spirit in their private worship sessions with the Lord.

PRAISE AND ITS USES
Praise is a form of worship in which we speak and sing words to God expressing our love and adoration for Him and give thanks to Him.

116

Praise has two main uses

(1) It can be used to serve and please God as it is in worship.
(2) It can be used as a weapon against the enemy (Satan and his cohorts) in the face of temptation.

PRAISE AS A WEAPON

In Psalms 8:2; 9:2-3 and 22:3, we are told God inhabits the praises of His people and uses it to still and stop the enemy and avenger, causing the enemy to fall and perish at His (God's) presence.

Psalm 8:2
Out of the mouth of babes and sucklings hast thou ordained strength because of thine enemies, that thou mightest still the enemy and the avenger.

Psalm 9:2-3
I will be glad and rejoice in thee: I will sing praise to thy name, O thou most High. When mine enemies are turned back, they shall fall and perish at thy presence.

Psalm 22:3
But thou art holy, O thou that inhabitest the praises of Israel.

However, praise that is going to be powerful must proceed from a heart that has received the light of God's Word guaranteeing victory over whatever problems one is facing. It is for this reason we see a pattern in God's Word of prayer preceding and mixed with praises. Prayer causes the Word of God that guarantees our victory to come into our hearts, and this hope causes us to praise God. We can see examples of this in Philippians 4:6-7; Acts 16:25-26.

Philippians 4:6-7
Be careful for nothing; but in everything by prayer and supplication with thanksgiving let your requests be made known unto God. And the peace of God, which passeth all understanding, shall keep your hearts and minds through Christ Jesus.

Acts 16: 25-26
And at midnight Paul and Silas prayed and sang praises unto God: and the prisoners heard them. And suddenly there was a great earthquake, so that the foundations of the prison were shaken: and immediately all the doors were opened, and every one's bands were loosed.

THE PROPER PLACE OF PRAISE
We see from the preceding scriptures that we cannot substitute praise for prayer, or, vice-versa. Each has its place. Praise proceeds from prayer. Prayer and meditation puts God's Word and power to work in our hearts. Praise comes out of our hearts that have God's Word and power in them.

When we face a problem, the first thing to do is seek God in prayer. During prayer we receive God's answer assuring us of help and deliverance. In the light of this assurance we then begin to praise God, before what we are trusting God for actually comes into manifestation. This praise is an act of faith.

Usually the manifestation of what we want comes during praise as God inhabits our praises. The answer to our prayers most times comes on the wings of praise. We can see this pattern in Acts 16:25-26 with Paul and Silas:

And at midnight Paul and Silas prayed, and sang praises unto God: and the prisoners heard them.
And suddenly there was a great earthquake, so that the foundations of the prison were shaken, and immediately all the doors were opened, and every one's bands were loosed.

We see this also with Jehoshaphat in 2 Chronicles 20:1-30. Here we see:

(i)   The problem in verses 1 & 2.
(ii)   Prayer (with fasting) in verses 3 - 13.
(iii)   God's answer of assurance in verses 14 - 17.
(iv)   Praise in response to God's answer before the manifestation in verses 18 & 19.
(v)   The answer and deliverance coming on the wings of praise in   verses 21 -   30.

This is a pattern we can follow to use praise as a weapon in the face of problems Satan brings into our lives, putting prayer and praise in their proper places.

Tabernacle of Moses

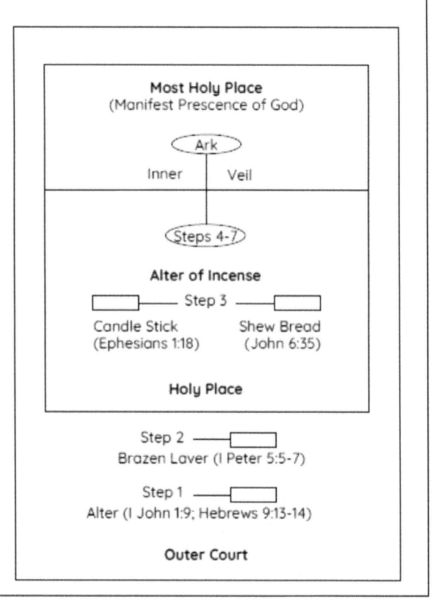

Most Holy Place
(Manifest Prescence of God)

Ark

Inner | Veil

Steps 4-7

Alter of Incense

Step 3

Candle Stick
(Ephesians 1:18)

Shew Bread
(John 6:35)

Holy Place

Step 2
Brazen Laver (I Peter 5:5-7)

Step 1
Alter (I John 1:9; Hebrews 9:13-14)

Outer Court

Appendix 1

This principle (these seven steps) is concealed in the tabernacle of Moses and in Ephesians 6:14-18:
1.   Girdle of truth (1John 1:8) Breastplate of righteousness (1 John 1:9) Step 1 (Ephesians 6:14).

2.   Feet shod with the preparation of the Gospel of Peace: Humility and Repentance (1Peter 5:5-7); Shield of Faith and Helmet of Salvation: Faith and Hope to receive grace from God (Ephesians 2:8) - Step 2   (Ephesians 6:15,16).

3.   Sword of the Spirit (The Word of God), which gives
        (i) Life (2Peter 1:4; Proverbs 18:20,21)
        (ii)Legal basis for prayer request John 16:23; Numbers 23:19) - Step 3 (Ephesians 6:17).
Praying always with all prayer and supplication in the Spirit (1Timothy 2:1-4; Hebrews 5:7) - Steps 4-7 (Ephesians 6:18)

SEVEN STEPS
(Proverbs 9:1; Psalms 37:23; 119:133)
CONCEALED IN THE TABERNACLE OF MOSES -
Hebrews 9:1-12; Exodus 25:9

The essence of prayer is to bring God's power and presence into physical manifestation. The High Priest under the Old Testament entered the Most Holy Place by following a set order. This order is a type or shadow of the way the New Testament saint should approach God in place of prayer to bring God's presence into physical manifestation (Romans 15:4; 1Corinthians 10:11; Hebrews 9:8-11).

Appendix   2

THE PRINCIPLES OF PERFECTION

Perfection* is a state in which the sin nature has been totally cleansed from the soul (mind, will and emotions) and the flesh, the physical body (2 Corinthians 7:1; Ephesians 5:26; Hebrews 10:22).

This does not mean you can no longer sin; however, the frequency and gravity of your sins will be drastically reduced.

Also, if and when you do sin quickly repent of and forsake the sin and maintain the state of perfection by a diligent walk in the Spirit (2 Peter 3:14; 1 Timothy 6:14)

In order to do this you must be a wise virgin (Matthew 25:2) operating consistently, daily, the seven pillars (or principles of wisdom (Proverbs 9: 1). These seven principles are:

1   The fear of the Lord which includes honesty and humility of heart through submission to divine authority.

2   Praying in the Spirit which includes praying with all types of prayer with travail (Hebrews 5: 7; Ephesians 6: 18) to overcome the power of the enemy to have victory each day; as well as communion prayer, which is speaking in tongues as frequently as possible (Jude 20) during daily, physical activities to acknowledge and have communion with the Holy Spirit (1Corinthians 14: 15, 18). Also to receive hidden wisdom of God and to have the mind of Christ (1Corinthians 2, 7, 10, 13, 16).

3   Binding the devil in the air (Matthew 18: 18) and taking the kingdom by force (Matthew 11: 12; Romans 14: 17).

4   Confessing the Word of God on the leading and the fruit of the Holy Spirit. (Romans 10:9 - 10) and on healing, prosperity etc.

5   Meditating on the Word of God, which means thinking on the Word, especially, the characteristics of divine love in 1Corinthians 13:4-8; Joshua 1:8, with a determination to practice it; and daily balanced bible reading.

6   The doing or daily practice of the word of God in everyday situations.

7   Fasting and prayer on a regular basis and living a fasted life. This means setting aside time on a weekly basis(Isaiah 58: 13) to proclaim a Sabbath, and also daily allowing the Holy Spirit to control what, when and how much you eat (Isaiah 7: 15; Ecclesiastes 10:16-17; Luke 21:34).

These seven principles form a cycle, because the seventh pillar, fasting and prayer and living a fasted life, makes you more humble (Psalms 35: 13) and so fearing God more, which is pillar number one.

Furthermore, these principles, applied daily, consistently and diligently will bring you over time, into the experience of cleansing perfection where the sin nature is totally removed from the soul and body (Luke 13: 32, Numbers 14:34).

*See our website www.spcconline.net for more information on perfection.

Also, access our articles by doing a search for olubijohnson on major search engines like 'Google.'

Appendix 3

PERFECTION (KINGDOM) SCRIPTURES FOR MEDITATION

Meditate: think on one perfection scripture daily so that you can gradually experience the reality of perfection (Proverbs 23:7; Genesis 30: 7-39).

Matthew 10:25; 11:28-29; 13:31-32,33; 22:36-40

Mark 4:26-29,30-32; 9:49.

Luke 6:40; 8:14-15; 9:23-27; 11:33-36; 13:18-21; 17:20-21; 18:17, 20:17-18; 21: 19, 36

John 8:12, 28-36; 10:10,15; 12:24-26; 14:10-13,20-23; 15:6; 17:3, 20-23

Acts 2:22; 6:8; 14:22

Romans 5:17; 6:6; 8:2; 11, 29; 12:1-2; 13:10.

I Corinthians 1:10, 2:6-16, 4:9-20; 9:24-27; 13:10-13; 16:13-14

2 Corinthians 3:18; 4:6-12; 5:4; 6:16-7:1; 13:9,11.

Galatians 2:20; 4:19; 5:5-6,14, 16-24; 6:14-16

Ephesians 3:16-20; 4:12-24, 30; 5:2, 26-27

Philippians 2:5-13; 3:10-16.

Colossians 1:27-29; 3:13-17; 4:12.

I Thessalonians 3:12-13; 5:8-9,23.

2 Thessalonians 1:10-12.

1 Timothy 1:5; 4:12-16; 6:11-15.

2 Timothy 2:10, 20-21; 3:16-17; 4:18.

Titus 2:11-14.

Hebrews 2:10-12; 4:9-16; 5:5-14; 6:1, 11-12; 7:11, 19, 26; 8:8-12; 9:12-15; 10:22, 35-39; 12:1-3, 11, 22, 28; 13:20-21.

James 1:2-4, 21-27; 2:8-13; 3:2, 13, 17-18; 5:7-8.

1 Peter 1:5,9,22-25; 4:1-2, 7-8, 12-13; 5:4-10.

2 Peter 1:2-10, 19; 3:11-15.

1 John 2:5-6; 3:1-3, 9; 4:12-18; 5:18-20

2 John 7, 8, 12.

3 John 2, 13, 14. Jude 24.

Revelation 1:10; 2:17, 24-28; 3:5, 12, 21; 14:1.

Appendix 4

THE MERCY PRINCIPLE

This is to make the yoke and the burden of praying and walking in the Spirit easier and lighter. For prayers, confessions and meditations that have already been made explicitly or completely at least once during a particular day (or 24 hour period- Gen.1:3-5); subsequent repetitions of such prayers, confessions and meditations can be replaced wholly or in part by the simple confession or meditation of:

"Lord have mercy on me (us) in this regard". The mercy of God so confessed or meditated by faith does the following at the same time.

Activates the high priestly ministry of Christ (Heb.2:17) to cleanse sin (I Jn.1:7; 2:2) and to give victory after judgement (Jam.2:13) and satanic accusation (Rev.12:10-11)

Gives living water (eternal life Jude 1:21). Covers for the omission of the extra spiritual effort (sacrifice, Heb.13:15, Mt.9:13) of your explicit (complete) confession and meditation. This omission makes the yoke and burden of confession and meditation easier and lighter (Mt.11:29-30) causing you to enter into a greater degree of God's rest (Heb.4:9-11). For this principle to work effectively, you must walk in honesty and humility of heart, forgiveness, and showing mercy unto others (Mt.5:7, 1Pet.5:5)

It is with this mercy principle that you can keep the law of life and love completely (24 hour daily) and thus gradually (Mk.4:28) do it perfectly.

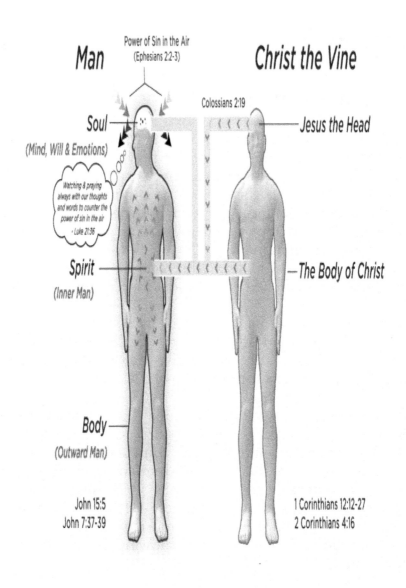

CPSIA information can be obtained
at www.ICGtesting.com
Printed in the USA
LVHW081316140420
653405LV00017B/1933